44 Letters from
the Liquid Modern World

44 Letters from the Liquid Modern World

Zygmunt Bauman

polity

Polity Press
65 Bridge Street
Cambridge CB2 1UR, UK

Polity Press
350 Main Street
Malden, MA 02148, USA

ISBN-13: 978-0-7456-5056-2 (hardback)
ISBN-13: 978-0-7456-5057-9 (paperback)

A catalogue record for this book is available from the British Library.

Typeset in 11 on 13 pt Sabon
by Toppan Best-set Premedia Limited
Printed and bound in Great Britain by the MPG Books Group

The publisher has used its best endeavours to ensure that the URLs for external websites referred to in this book are correct and active at the time of going to press. However, the publisher has no responsibility for the websites and can make no guarantee that a site will remain live or that the content is or will remain appropriate.

Every effort has been made to trace all copyright holders, but if any have been inadvertently overlooked the publisher will be pleased to include any necessary credits in any subsequent reprint or edition.

For further information on Polity, visit our website:
www.politybooks.com

Contents

On writing letters – from a liquid modern world

Letters from the liquid modern world . . . This is what the editors of *La Repubblica delle Donne* asked me to write and send to its readers once a fortnight – and what I have been doing for almost two years (2008 and 2009; they are collected here in an edited and somewhat extended version).

From the 'liquid modern' world: that means from the world you and I, the writer of forthcoming letters and their possible/probable/hoped for readers, share. The world I call 'liquid' because, like all liquids, it cannot stand still and keep its shape for long. Everything or almost everything in this world of ours keeps changing: fashions we follow and the objects of our attention (constantly shifting attention, today drawn away from things and events that attracted it yesterday, and to be drawn away tomorrow from things and events that excite us today), things we dream of and things we fear, things we desire and things we loathe, reasons to be hopeful and reasons to be apprehensive. And the conditions around us, conditions in which we make our living and try to plan our future, in which we connect to some people and disconnect (or are disconnected) from others, keep changing as well. Opportunities for more happiness and threats of misery flow or float by, come and go and change places, and more often than not they do all that too swiftly and nimbly to allow us to do something sensible and effective to direct or redirect them, keep them on course or forestall them.

To cut a long story short: this world, our liquid modern world, keeps surprising us: what seems certain and proper today may well appear futile, fanciful or a regrettable mistake tomorrow. We suspect that this may happen, so we feel that – like the world that is our home – we, its residents, and intermittently its designers, actors, users and casualties, need to be constantly ready to change: we all need to be, as the currently fashionable word suggests, 'flexible'. So we crave more information about what is going on and what is likely to happen. Fortunately, we now have what our parents could not even imagine: we have the internet and the world-wide web, we have 'information highways' connecting us promptly, 'in real time', to every nook and cranny of the planet, and all that inside these handy pocket-size mobile phones or iPods, within our reach day and night and moving wherever we do. Fortunately? Alas, perhaps not that fortunately after all, since the bane of insufficient information that made our parents suffer has been replaced by the yet more awesome bane of a flood of information which threatens to drown us and makes swimming or diving (as distinct from drifting or surfing) all but impossible. How to sift the news that counts and matters from the heaps of useless and irrelevant rubbish? How to derive meaningful messages from senseless noise? In the hubbub of contradictory opinions and suggestions we seem to lack a threshing machine that might help us separate the grains of truth and of the worthwhile from the chaff of lies, illusion, rubbish and waste . . .

In these letters, I'll try to do just what the threshing machine (absent now, alas, and probably for some time) would have done for us had it been in our possession: to begin, at least, to separate the important from the insubstantial, things that matter – and are likely to matter more and more – from false alarms and flashes in the pan. But since, as mentioned before, this liquid modern world of ours is constantly on the move, we all are willy-nilly, knowingly or not, joyfully or plaintively, perpetually carried along in travel even if we try to stay still and hold on to one place. The letters, therefore, could not be other than 'travel reports' – even though their author has not budged from Leeds, the city in which he lives; and the stories they will be telling will be travelogues: stories from and of travels.

Walter Benjamin, a philosopher with an eye uniquely sharpened to spot any hints of logic and system in apparently diffuse and random cultural tremors, used to distinguish between two types of stories: sailors' stories and peasants' stories. The first are tales of things bizarre and unheard of, of far-away places, never visited and probably never to be visited, of monsters and mutants, witches and sorcerers, gallant knights and scheming evil-doers – people jarringly different from the people listening to the story of their exploits, and doing things which other people (particularly those who listen, enchanted and bewitched, to the sailor's tale) would never contemplate or imagine doing, let alone dare to do. Peasants' stories, on the contrary, are tales of ordinary, close-by and apparently familiar events, like the ever-repeated annual cycle of seasons or the daily chores of the household, farm and field. I said *apparently* familiar, since the impression of knowing such things thoroughly, inside out, and therefore expecting there to be nothing new to be learned from and about them, is also an illusion – in this case coming precisely from their being too close to the eye to see them clearly for what they are. Nothing escapes scrutiny so nimbly, resolutely and stubbornly as 'things at hand', things 'always there', 'never changing'. They are, so to speak, 'hiding in the light' – the light of deceptive and misleading familiarity! Their ordinariness is a blind, discouraging all scrutiny. To make them into objects of interest and close examination they must first be cut off and torn away from that sense-blunting, cosy yet vicious cycle of routine quotidianity. They must first be set aside and kept at a distance before scanning them properly can become conceivable: the bluff of their alleged 'ordinariness' must be called at the start. And then the mysteries they hide, profuse and profound mysteries – those turning strange and puzzling once you start thinking about them – can be laid bare and explored.

The distinction made by Benjamin almost a century ago is no longer as clear-cut as it originally was: sailors no longer have a monopoly on visiting bizarre lands, while in a globalized world in which no place is really separate and secure from the impact of every and any other place on the planet, however far away it might be, even the tales told by an erstwhile peasant may be difficult to distinguish from a sailor's story. Well, what I am going to try for in my letters will be, so to speak, *sailors'* stories as told by *peasants*. Tales drawn from the most ordinary lives, but as a way to reveal and expose the extraordinariness we would otherwise overlook. If we wish them to become truly *familiar*, apparently familiar things need first to be made *strange*.

This is a difficult task. Most certainly, success is anything but guaranteed, whereas full success is, to say the least, highly doubtful. But this is the task which we, the writer and the readers of these 44 letters, shall try to pursue in our shared adventure.

But why 44? Does the selecting of this number rather than any other have a special meaning of its own, or has it been an accidental, arbitrary decision, a random choice? I suspect that most readers (perhaps all of them, unless they are Polish . . .) would ask the question. I owe them some explanation.

The greatest of Polish romantic poets, Adam Mickiewicz, conjured up a mysterious figure, a blend or a hybrid of, on one hand, a plenipotentiary of Freedom, its spokesman, holder of its power of attorney, and, on the other, its governor or vice-regent on earth. 'His name is Forty-Four': this is how that recondite creature was introduced by one of the characters in Mickiewicz's poem in his announcement/premonition of its imminent arrival. But why that name? Many historians of literature, immensely better equipped to find an answer than myself, have tried in vain to crack that mystery. Some have suggested that the choice is the sum of the numerical values of the letters in the poet's name if written in Hebrew – perhaps an allusion, simultaneously, to the poet's high stature in Poland's struggle for liberation and the Jewish origin of the poet's mother. The most widely accepted interpretation, though, thus far has been that Mickiewicz chose that sonorously, majestic-sounding phrase (in Polish: *czterdzieści i cztery*) simply in the heat of inspiration – motivated (if not altogether unmotivated, as most flashes of inspiration tend to be) by a care for poetic harmony rather than an intention to convey a cryptic message.

The letters collected here under a single cover have been composed over a period of almost two years: How many of them should there be? When and where to stop? The impulse to write letters from the liquid modern world is unlikely ever to be exhausted – that kind of world, pulling ever new surprises out of its sleeve, daily inventing new challenges to human understanding, will see to it that it isn't. Surprises and challenges are scattered all over the spectrum of human experience – and so every stopping point for reporting them in letters, and by the same token limiting their range, must inevitably be arbitrarily chosen. These letters are no exception. Their number has been arbitrarily chosen.

Why this number, though, and not any other? Because the 44 figure, thanks to Adam Mickiewicz, has been made to stand for the awe of, and hope for, the arrival of Freedom. And so this number signals, if in an oblique manner and only to the initiated, the guiding motif of these missives. The spectre of freedom is present in every one of these 44 otherwise thematically varied letters – even when, as is the nature of spectres true to their name, invisibly.

Crowded solitude

On the website of the *Chronicle of Higher Education* (http://chronicle.com) you could read recently about a teenage girl who sent 3,000 text messages in one month. That means she sent on average a hundred messages a day, or about one every ten waking minutes – 'morning, noon, and night, weekdays and weekends, class time, lunchtime, homework time, and toothbrushing time'. What follows is that she's hardly ever been alone for more than ten minutes: that means she has never been just *with herself* – with her thoughts, her dreams, her worries and hopes. By now, she's probably forgotten how one lives – thinks, does things, laughs or cries – in one's own company, without the company of others. Or, more to the point, she has never had a chance to learn that art. As a matter of fact, it is only in her incapacity to practise that art that she is not alone . . .

The pocket-size gadgets sending and receiving messages are not the sole tools needed by that girl and others like her to survive without that art. Professor Jonathan Zimmerman of New York University notes that up to three out of four American teens spend every minute of their available time glued to the websites of Facebook or MySpace: chatting. They are, he suggests, hooked on making and receiving electronic noises or screen flashes. The chat websites are, Zimmerman says, new potent drugs to which teens are now addicted. You've heard about the withdrawal torments of people, young and not so young alike, addicted to other kinds of drugs; you can therefore imagine the agony those teens would go through were some virus (or their parents, or their teachers) to block their internet connections or put their mobiles out of operation.

In our unpredictable, constantly surprising and stubbornly unfamiliar world, the prospect of being left alone may indeed feel horrifying; one can name a lot of reasons to conceive of solitude as a highly uncomfortable, threatening and terrifying condition. It would be as unjust as it is silly to blame electronics alone for what is happening to people born into a world woven from cabled, wired or wireless connectivity. Electronic contraptions answer a need not of their own making; the most they could have done was render a need already fully formed yet more acute and salient, as the ways of acting on it have come tantalizingly within everybody's reach, and call for no more effort than pushing a few keys. Inventors and sellers of 'Walkmans', the first mobile gadgets allowing you to 'hear the world' whenever and wherever you wished, promised their clients: 'Never again (will you be) alone!' Obviously, they knew what they were talking about, and why that advertising slogan was likely to sell the gadgets on offer – as it did, in uncounted millions. They knew there were millions of people in the streets who felt lonely, and who detested their solitude as painful and abhorrent; people not just deprived of company, but grieving over its absence. With ever more family homes empty during the day, and with family hearths and dining tables replaced by TV sets in every room – with people, we may say, 'each trapped in their own cocoon' – fewer and fewer people could count on the enlivening and invigorating warmth of human company; though without company they did not know how to fill their hours and days.

Dependence on uninterrupted Walkman-emitted noise only deepened that void left behind by the vanishing company. And the longer they stayed sunk in that void, the less they were able to use the means before high-tech, such as their own muscles and imagination, to climb out of it. With the arrival of the internet, that void could also be forgotten or covered up, and thereby detoxified; at least the pain it caused could be assuaged. That company that had all too often been missing, and was increasingly being missed, seemed to have returned, though through electronic screens rather than wooden doors, and in a new analogue or digital – but in both cases virtual – incarnation: people scrambling out of the torments of loneliness found this new form to be a considerable improvement on the vanished face-to-face and hand-in-hand variety. With the skills of face-to-face interaction largely forgotten or never learned, all or almost all of what might have been resented as a shortcoming of online, virtual 'connecting' was widely welcomed as an advantage. What Facebook, MySpace and their like offered has been greeted as the best of both worlds. Or so, at least, it seemed to people who longed desperately for human company yet felt ill at ease, inept and hapless when they found themselves among it.

To start with, there is no longer any need, ever again, to be alone. Every minute – 24 hours a day, seven days a week – it takes just one push of a button to conjure up company out of a collection of loners. In that online world, no one is ever away, everyone seems to be constantly at one's beck and call – and even if she or he accidentally falls asleep, there are enough others to send a message to, or just twitter for a few seconds, for the temporary absence to pass unnoticed. Secondly, 'contact' may be made with other people without necessarily initiating an exchange that would threaten giving hostages to fate, taking a course one might not enjoy. 'Contact' can be broken at the first sign of the exchange taking a turn in an unwelcome direction: no risk therefore, and also no need to find excuses, apologise and lie; a gossamer-light touch of the finger, totally painless and risk-free, will suffice. There is neither any need to be afraid of being alone, nor a threat of exposure to other people's demands, of a demand for sacrifice or compromise, of having to do something you don't feel like doing just because others wish you to do so. That comforting awareness can be retained and enjoyed even when you are sitting in a crowded room, loitering in the densely packed passageways of a shopping mall, or strolling on the street among a large pack of friends and fellow-strollers; you can always 'make yourself spiritually absent' and be 'on your own', as well as notify the others around you that you are willing, here and now, to stay out of touch; you can put yourself outside the crowd by keeping your fingers busy kneading a message to someone who is physically absent and therefore momentarily undemanding and unengaging, safe to 'contact', or by glancing over a message just received from such a person. With such gadgets in your hand, you could even make yourself alone inside a stampeding herd if you wished to; and instantly – the moment the company crowds you and gets too oppressive for your taste. You don't swear loyalty till death do you part, and you can expect everyone else to be 'available' whenever you need them, without, however, having to bear the unsavoury consequences of being constantly available to others . . .

So paradise on earth? Dream coming true, at long last? The admittedly haunting ambivalence of human interaction – comforting and exhilarating, yet cumbersome and full of pitfalls – finally resolved? Opinions on that matter stay divided. What seems beyond dispute, however, is that there is a price to pay for all that – a price that may prove, if you think about it, too high to be willingly paid. Because once you are 'always on', you may never be fully and truly alone. And if you are never alone, then (to quote Professor Zimmerman once more), 'you're less likely to read a book for pleasure, to draw a picture, to stare out the window and imagine worlds others than your own . . . You're less likely to communicate with the real people in your immediate surroundings. Who wants to talk to family members when your friends are just a click away?' (and they come in inexhaustible numbers and fascinating variety; there are, let me add, five hundred or more Facebook 'friends').

Running away from *loneliness*, you drop your chance of *solitude* on the way: of that sublime condition in which one can 'gather thoughts', ponder, reflect, create – and so, in the last account, give meaning and substance to communication. But then, having never savoured its taste, you may never know what you have forfeited, dropped and lost.

3
Parents and children conversing

On the origins of one of his remarkable short stories, 'Averroes' Search', the great Argentinean writer Jorge Luis Borges said that in it he tried 'to narrate the process of failure', of 'defeat' – as when a theologian seeks the final, irrefutable proof of God's existence, an alchemist seeks the philosopher's stone, a technology buff seeks a perpetuum mobile, or a mathematician searches for the way to square a circle. But then he decided that 'a more poetic case' would be one 'of a man who sets himself a goal that is not forbidden to others, but is to him'. He picked the case of Averroes, the great Muslim philosopher, who set out to translate Aristotle's *Poetics*, but 'bounded within the circle of Islam, could never know the meaning of the words *tragedy* and *comedy*'. Indeed, 'without ever having suspected what theatre is', Averroes would be bound, inescapably, to fail when trying 'to imagine what a play is'.

As a topic for a wonderful story told by a great writer, the case finally selected by Borges proves indeed 'more poetic'. But if looked at from the less inspired, mundane and rather humdrum sociological perspective, it looks, rather, fairly *prosaic*. Only a few intrepid souls try to construct a perpetuum mobile or find the philosopher's stone; but trying in vain to understand what others have no difficulty in understanding is an experience we all know only too well from personal observation, and learn again daily – more perhaps now, in the twenty-first century, than our ancestors did in times past. Look at just one example: communicating with your children, if you are a parent. Or with your parents, if you haven't yet missed that chance ...

Mutual incomprehension between generations, 'old' and 'young', and the reciprocal suspicion that follows it have a long history. One can easily trace symptoms of such suspicion to quite ancient times. But intergenerational suspicion has become much more salient in our *modern* era, marked by continuous profound and accelerated changes in life conditions. The radical acceleration of the pace of change characteristic of modern times, in stark opposition to centuries of interminable reiteration and sluggish change, allowed the fact of 'things changing' and 'things being no longer as they used to be' to be experienced personally and personally noted, in the course of a single human life. Such awareness implied an association (or even a causal link) between changes in the human condition and the departure of older generations and the arrival of newer ones.

And once that implication existed, it became noticeable and was presumed to be obvious that (at least since the beginning of modernity and through its duration) age cohorts entering the world at different stages of the continuous transformation tended indeed to *differ* sharply in the evaluation of the life conditions they *shared*. Children as a rule enter a world drastically different from the one their parents remember from their own childhood years and which they were trained and accustomed to take as a standard of 'normality'; they, the children, will never visit that other, vanished world of their parents' youth. What may be seen as 'natural' by some age cohorts, as 'the way things *are*', 'the way things are *normally done*' and thus '*ought* to be done', can be viewed by another as an aberration: as a departure from the norm, bizarre and perhaps also as an illegitimate and unreasonable state of affairs – unfair, abominable, contemptible or ludicrous, and crying out for a thorough revision. What to some age cohorts may seem a comfortable and cosy condition, allowing learned and mastered skills and routines to be deployed, may appear odd and off-putting to another; whereas people of a different age may feel in their element in situations which make the other people feel ill at ease, baffled and at a loss.

The differences of perception have become so multifaceted by now that, unlike in premodern times, younger people no longer are cast by older generations as 'miniature adults' or 'would-be adults' – not as 'beings not yet fully mature but bound to mature' ('mature' being read as 'being like us'). Nowadays, youngsters are not hoped or supposed to be 'on the way to becoming adult *like us*', but viewed as a rather *different kind* of people, bound to *remain* different 'from us' throughout their lives. The differences between 'us' (the older ones) and 'them' (the younger ones) no longer feel like temporary irritants destined to dissolve and evaporate as the youngsters (inevitably) wise up to the realities of life. They are bound to stay; they are irrevocable.

As a result, the older and the younger age cohorts tend to eye each other with a mixture of miscomprehension and misapprehension. The older ones will fear that the newcomers to the world are about to spoil and destroy that familiar, comfortable, decent 'normality' which they, their elders, have laboriously built and preserved with loving care; the younger ones, on the contrary, will feel an acute urge to put right what the ageing veterans have botched and made a mess of. Both will be unsatisfied (or at least not fully satisfied) with the current state of affairs and the direction in which their world seems to be moving – and blame the other side for their discomfort. In two consecutive issues of a widely respected British weekly, two jarringly different assertions/ assessments were made public: a columnist accused 'the young people' of being 'bovine, lazy-arsed, chlamydia stuffed and good for nothing', to which a reader angrily responded that the allegedly slothful and uncaring youngsters are in fact 'academically high-achieving' and 'concerned about the mess that adults have created'.[1] Here, as in uncountable other similar disagreements, the difference was clearly between *evaluations* and subjectively coloured *viewpoints*. In cases like this, the resulting controversy can hardly be 'objectively' resolved.

But let's also remember that the bulk of the presently young generation have never experienced real hardship, long and prospectless economic depression and mass unemployment. They were born and grew up in a world in which they could shelter under a socially produced and communally serviced, waterproof and windproof umbrella that seemed to remain forever at their disposal and within their reach to protect them against inclement weather, cold rains and freezing winds – and in a world in which every next morning was hoped/expected to be a day sunnier than the last and more lavishly sprinkled with pleasant adventures. As

I write these words, however, dark clouds gather over that world, getting darker by the day. The happy condition, sanguine and full of promise, which the young came to believe to be the 'natural' state of the world, may not last much longer. The sediment of the last economic depression – protracted unemployment, rapidly shrinking life chances and darkening life prospects – may refuse to be washed away quickly, if ever; and sunny and consistently sunnier days are not at all certain to return fast – if at all.

And so it is too early to decide how the ingrained worldviews and attitudes of the present-day young will eventually fit the world to come, and how that world will fit their ingrained expectations.

4
Offline, online

Ann-Sophie, a 20-year-old student at the Copenhagen Business School, replied to questions set by Flemming Wisler: 'I don't want my life to control me too much. I don't want to sacrifice everything to my career . . . The most important thing is to be comfortable . . . Nobody wants to be stuck in the same job for long.'[2] In other words: Keep your options wide open. Don't swear loyalty of a 'till death do us part' kind – to anything or anybody. The world is full of wondrous, seductive and promising chances; it would be a folly to miss any of them by tying your hands and feet with irrevocable commitments . . .

There is no wonder that *surfing* figures high on the list of basic life skills which the young are prompted to acquire and seek, and are eager to master, above the increasingly old-fashioned 'sounding' and 'fathoming'. But, as Katie Baldo, guidance counsellor of the Cooperstown Middle School in New York State, has noted, 'Teens are missing some major social cues because they are too engrossed in their iPods, cell phones, or video games. I see it all the time in the halls when they can't voice a hello or make eye contact.'[3] Making eye contact and thereby acknowledging the physical proximity of another human being spells waste: it portends the necessity of spending a portion of precious yet loathsomely scarce time on deep diving (something which the exploration of depths would most certainly demand); a decision that would interrupt or pre-empt surfing over so many other, no less, if not more, inviting surfaces.

In a life of continuous emergency, *virtual* relations easily beat the '*real* stuff'. Whereas it is primarily the offline world that prompts young men and women to be constantly on the move, such pressures would be to no avail were it not for the electronically based capacity to multiply encounters between individuals by making them brief, shallow and eminently disposable. Virtual relations are equipped with 'delete' and 'spam' keys that protect against the cumbersome (above all, time-consuming) consequences of in-depth interaction. One can't help recalling Chance (a character played by Peter Sellers in Hal Ashby's film of 1979, *Being There*): having emerged into a busy town street from his protracted and exclusive *tête-à-tête* with the world-as-seen-on-TV, he tries in vain to remove an unnerving and discomforting bevy of nuns from his vision with the help of his hand-held pilot.

For the young, the main attraction of the virtual world derives from the absence of the contradictions and cross-purposes that haunt offline life. Unlike its offline alternative, the online world renders an infinite multiplication of contacts conceivable – both plausible and feasible. It does this through reducing their duration and, consequently, by *weakening* such bonds as call for, and often enforce duration – in stark opposition to its offline counterpart, which is known to find its bearings in a continuous effort to *strengthen* bonds by severely limiting the number of contacts while extending and deepening each of them. This is a genuine advantage for men and women who would torment themselves with the thought that a step they have taken might (just might) have been a mistake, and that it might (just might) be too late for them to cut their losses. Hence the resentment towards everything redolent of a 'long-term' commitment – be it planning one's life, or one's engagements with other living beings. Evidently appealing to the younger generation's values, a recent commercial announced the arrival of a new mascara that 'vows to stay pretty for 24 hours', and commented: 'Talk about a committed relationship. One stroke and these pretty lashes last through rain, sweat, humidity, tears. Yet the formula removes easily with warm water' – 24 hours already feels like a 'committed relationship', but even so brief a 'commitment' wouldn't be an attractive choice if its consequences weren't so childishly easy to remove.

Whatever choice is eventually made will be reminiscent of the 'light cloak' of Max Weber, one of the founders of modern sociology; it could be shaken off the shoulders at will, instantly and without much ado – unlike his 'steel casing', which offered effective and lasting protection against turbulence but was also difficult to get rid off, as well as cramping the movement of the person it protected and severely constricting the space for the exercise of that person's free will. What matters most for the young is to retain the ability to *reshape* 'identity' and the 'network' the moment a need (or, indeed, a whim) to reshape them arises or is suspected to have arrived. The worry of their ancestors about their one-off *identification* is increasingly elbowed out by a worry about perpetual *reidentification*. Identities must be *disposable*; an unsatisfying or not-sufficiently-satisfying identity, or an identity betraying its advanced age, needs to be *easy to abandon*; perhaps biodegradability would be the ideal attribute of the identity most strongly desired nowadays.

The interactive capacities of the internet are made to the measure of this new need. In their internet-enabled rendering, it is the *quantity* of connections rather than their *quality* that makes all the difference between the chances of success or failure. That rendering makes it possible to stay *au courant* with the latest talk of the town, and the choices made into 'musts' by that talk: the hits currently most listened to, the latest T-shirt designs, the latest exploits of the hottest celebrities of the day, the most recent and most commonly talked about parties, festivals and events in focus. Simultaneously, it helps in updating the contents and redistributing the emphases in the portrayal of one's self; it also helps in swiftly effacing the traces of the past, the now shamefully outdated contents and emphases. All in all, the internet greatly facilitates, prompts and even necessitates the incessant labours of *reinvention* – to an extent unachievable in offline life. This is arguably one of the most important reasons for the time spent by the 'electronic generation' in the virtual universe: time steadily growing at the expense of time lived in the 'real' (offline) world.

The referents of main concepts known to frame and map the *Lebenswelt*, the world as lived and lived-through, the *personally experienced* world of the young, are gradually yet steadily transplanted from the offline to the online world. Concepts like 'contacts', 'dates', 'meeting', 'communicating', 'community' or 'friendship' – all referring to interpersonal relations and social bonds – are the most prominent among such concepts. One of the foremost effects of the new location of referents is the perception of current social bonds and commitments as momentary snapshots in the ongoing process of renegotiation, rather than as steady states bound to last indefinitely. (But let me note right away that a 'momentary snapshot' is not a wholly felicitous metaphor: though 'momentary', snapshots may still imply more durability than the electronically mediated bonds and commitments possess. The word 'snapshot' belongs to the vocabulary of photographic prints and photographic paper, which can only accept one image in their lifetime – whereas for electronic ties *effacing* and *re*writing or *over*writing, inconceivable in the case of celluloid negatives and photographic papers, are the most important and most resorted to options; indeed, they are the only indelible attribute of electronically mediated ties.)

5

As the birds do

'Twitter' is what birds produce when they tweet. And as the experts in bird life will tell you, tweeting plays two roles in the life of birds, apparently at odds, but equally vital: it allows them to keep in touch with each other (that is, prevents them from being lost, or from losing track of their partners in the nest or the rest of the flock), and to prevent other birds, and particularly other birds of the same species, from transgressing on the territory they've made or intend to make their own. Birds' twitter has no other message to convey, and so its 'contents' (even if it had any, which it does not) would be irrelevant; what counts is that the familiar sound has been made, and could be (hopefully *will* be) heard.

I can't say whether Jack Dorsey, who founded the website called 'Twitter' in 2006, when he was still in his student years, did or didn't take inspiration from a bird habit hundreds of millions of years old. But the 55 million monthly visitors to that website seem to have followed that habit – knowingly or not. And they seem to have found it quite useful for their own needs and purposes. As Peder Zane of the *News and Observer* calculated on 15 March 2009, the number of Twitter users grew last year by 900 per cent (while the number of Facebook users grew, according to Wikipedia, by 'only' 228 per cent). The managers of the Twitter website invite and encourage newcomers to join the 55-million strong army of present users by pointing out that 'Twitter is a service for friends, family, and co-workers to communicate and stay connected through the exchange of quick, frequent answers to one simple question: What are you doing?' Answers, as you surely know, must be not only quick and frequent, but easy to digest, and that means very, very compact and short (just like the tunes of a bird's twitter) – no longer than 140 characters. So that 'doing' on which you can tweet may mean not much more than 'having a quatro formaggio pizza', or 'looking through the window', or 'feeling sleepy and going to bed', or 'being dead bored'. Courtesy of the Twitter management, our notorious yet shameful reticence and awkwardness in reporting the motives and the goals of our actions, and the feelings that accompany them, have been acquitted of being a handicap and promoted to the rank of a virtue. What we, along with all the other people like us, are told and given to understand is that the only thing that matters is to know and to make others know what we are doing – at this moment or any other; what matters is 'to be in view'. Why we are doing it and what we are thinking, aiming at, dreaming of, enjoying or regretting when we are doing it, or even the other reasons that inspired us to tweet apart from wishing to manifest our presence, do not really matter.

Once face-to-face contact is replaced by a screen-to-screen variety, it is the *surfaces* that come into touch. Courtesy of Twitter, 'surfing', the preferred means of locomotion in our hurried life of instantly born and instantly vanishing opportunities, has finally caught up with interhuman communication. What has suffered as a result is the intimacy, the depth and the durability of human intercourse and human bonds.

The promoters and enthusiasts of faster, easier, trouble-free 'contacts' (more precisely: the reconfirmation of 'being connected') try to convince us that the gains more than compensate for the losses. Under the heading of 'uses' (of tweeting) we learn, for instance, from Wikipedia that 'during the 2008 Mumbai attacks, eyewitnesses sent an estimated 80 tweets every five seconds as the tragedy unfolded. Twitter users on the ground helped in compiling a list of the dead and injured'; that 'in January 2009, US Airways Flight 1549 experienced multiple bird strikes and had to be ditched in the Hudson River after takeoff from LaGuardia Airport in New York City. Janis Krums, a passenger on one of the ferries that rushed to help, took a picture of the downed plane as passengers

were still evacuating and tweeted it via *TwitPic* before traditional
media arrived at the scene'; or that 'in February 2009, the Australian *Country Fire Authority* used Twitter to send out regular
alerts and updates regarding the *2009 Victorian bushfires*'. But
expounding on such cases is like trying to convince would-be lotto
punters of the universal benefits of buying lottery tickets by publishing from time to time the smiling likenesses of the few jackpot
winners – while avoiding mentioning the millions of frustrated
losers . . .

Let's face it: the impact of the changing technology of human
communication is like the accomplishments of the bank-led
economy in that gains tend to be privatized while losses are
nationalized. And in both cases, 'collateral damage' is likely to be
disproportionately more widespread, profound and insidious than
the rare, occasional benefits.

There is, though, a benefit of a different kind, a much more
widespread benefit, which seems to be the prime attraction of
using the Twitter website. For some time now, Descartes's famous
'proof of existing', 'I think therefore I am', has been elbowed out
and chased away by a version updated for our era of mass communication: 'I am seen, therefore I am'. The more people can (and
may choose to) see me, the more convincing is the proof of my
own being here . . . The pattern is set by celebrities. You do not
measure the gravity and the weightiness of celebrities' presence by
the gravity of what have they *done* – the weightiness of their *deeds*
(you wouldn't anyway be able to properly evaluate those qualities
and to sufficiently trust your results to hold to the opinion you've
formed); you can be sure that 'celebrities' matter only because of
the obtrusiveness of their presence: they must be looked at and be
seen by myriads of people – on every news-stand, the front pages
of tabloids, the covers of glossy magazines, TV screens . . . If so
many people look at them, watch their every step, listen to every
bit of gossip about their latest exploits, mischiefs and pranks, talk
about them, then there must be something 'in it' – so many people
can't be simultaneously wrong! As Daniel Boorstin memorably
summed it all up: 'The celebrity is a person who is known for his
well-knownness.' Conclusion (not necessarily true, but credible all
the same)? The more frequently I tweet, and the more people visit
the site on which my tweeting is done, the more chances I'll
have of joining the ranks of those well-known. As in the case of

celebrities, it is really irrelevant what my tweeting is about. After all, what we read and hear about celebs is more often than not the latest news about their breakfasts, dates, one-night stands and shopping escapades. And since the weight of a person's presence in the world is measured by her or his 'well-knownness', my tweeting is also a way to increase my spiritual weightiness (a sort of dieting in reverse – dieting being seen as the method to decrease one's bodily weight).

Or so it seems at least. All that may be an illusion, but to many of our contemporaries it is a welcome illusion. Welcome to people drilled and instructed to believe that to *matter* comes from being *seen*, yet who are denied access to the glossy magazines and the tabloids that have the real power to divide people into the 'seen' and the invisible, and to keep them on the 'seeable' side of the division. Twitter is for us, the *ordinary* folks, what the covers of glossy weeklies and monthlies are for those few proclaimed *extraordinary*. Our twitter is like a high-street shop's replica of haute couture boutique splendours: the equality substitute for the deprived. To those doomed to high-street shopping, twitter mitigates the pangs of humiliation caused by the inaccessibility of exclusive boutiques.

6

Virtual sex

Emily Dubberley, author of *Brief Encounters: The Women's Guide to Casual Sex*, remarks that getting sex is now 'like ordering a pizza . . . Now you can just go online and order genitalia.' Flirting or making passes are no longer needed, there is no need either to work hard for a partner's approval, no need to lean over backwards in order to deserve and earn a partner's consent, to ingratiate oneself in her or his eyes, and to wait a long time, perhaps infinitely, for all those efforts to bring fruit.

That means, though, that gone are all those things that used to make a sexual encounter such an exiting, because uncertain, event, and seeking such an event such a romantic adventure, risky and full of traps. Gains hardly ever come pure, unaccompanied by losses. Internet-mediated sex, welcomed enthusiastically by so many users, is no exception to that sombre rule. Something has been lost – though many men, and almost as many women, are heard to be saying that what has been gained is worth the sacrifice. What has been gained, is *convenience* – cutting effort to an absolute minimum; *speed* – shortening the distance between desire and its satisfaction; and *insurance against consequences* – which, as is the habit of consequences, does not always follow the desired, pre-scripted scenario. Consequences are seldom fully anticipated, coveted and welcome. They can prove to be discomforting and vexing as often as they happen to be blissful and cloudlessly enjoyable.

One website offering the prospect of quick and safe ('no strings attached') sex, and boasting 2.5 million registered members, advertises itself with the slogan: 'Meet real sex partners *tonight!*' (italics added). Another, with millions of members around the world, profiled mostly to the wishes of the globetrotting part of the gay public, chose another slogan: 'What you want, *when* you want it' (italics added). There is a message only barely hidden in both slogans: the sought-after products are ready for consumption, instantaneous consumption, on the spot; desire is in a package deal with its gratification; it is you who are in charge. That message is sweet and soothing to ears trained by millions of commercials (each one of us is forced/manoeuvred into watching more commercials in one year than our grandparents would have seen in their whole lifetime). Those commercials now (unlike in our grandparents' time) promise sexual joys as instant as coffee or powdered soup ('just pour on hot water'), and degrade, condemn or ridicule the spatially or temporally remote joys that cannot be reached without patience, self-sacrifice and a lot of good will, long and arduous training, awkward, cumbersome and sometimes excruciatingly difficult efforts – and that portend as many errors as the trials they make necessary.

This sort of 'impatience complex' was encapsulated a few decades ago in Margaret Thatcher's memorable complaint against the National Health Service, and her explanation of why she thought a free market for medical services to be an improvement: 'I want a doctor of my choice, at the time of my choice.' Shortly afterwards the tools – magic wands in the shape of a credit card – were invented, if not to make Thatcher's dream come exactly true, then at least to render it plausible and credible. The tools brought the consumerist life philosophy within reach of a growing number of individuals whom banks and credit companies considered to be deserving of their attention and benevolence.

Ancient and non-temporal folk wisdom advises us 'not to count your chickens before they are hatched'. Well, the chickens of the new life strategy of instant joy have now been hatched in great profusion, a whole generation of them, and we have every right to start counting them. One such counting has been performed by psychotherapist Phillip Hodson, and his conclusions present the outcome of the internet phase of the ongoing sexual revolution as a rather mixed blessing. Hodson spotted the paradox of what he calls the 'throwaway, instant gratification culture' (not universal yet, but fast expanding): people who in a single evening may flirt (electronically) with more people than their parents, not to mention their grandparents, could in their entire lives find out sooner or later that, as in the case of all other addictions, the satisfaction they gain shrinks with every new dose of the drug. Were they to look closely at the evidence their experience supplied, they would have also found out – retrospectively, much to their surprise and frustration, though beyond the proverbial point of no return – that the long romance and slow and intricate seduction they can now only read about in old novels were not unnecessary, redundant, burdensome and irritating *obstacles* cluttering the way to the 'thing itself' (as they were made to believe), but important, perhaps even crucial, *ingredients* of that 'thing', indeed of *all* things erotic and 'sexy', of their charm and attraction.

In a nutshell: greater *quantity* has been acquired at the cost of *quality*. The 'new and improved', internet-mediated rendition of sex is, simply, not that 'thing' which fascinated and enamoured our ancestors so much that it inspired them to scribble volumes of poetry in order to praise its magnificence and glory, and to confuse marital bliss with heaven. And what Hodson, in agreement with a multitude of other researchers, found out as well is that rather than helping to tie human bonds and to cut down on the sum total of the tragedies of unfulfilled dreams, internet-mediated sex results in stripping human partnerships of much of their allure and cuts down on the number of dreams. Those bonds tied with the internet's help tend to be weaker and more superficial than those laboriously built in real 'offline' life, and for those reasons they are less (if at all) satisfying and coveted, less, if at all, 'valuable' – and valued.

As Georg Simmel pointed out a long time ago, the value of things is measured by the size of the sacrifice needed to obtain them. More people can now 'have sex' more often, but in parallel with the growth of those numbers, the numbers also grow of people living alone, suffering from loneliness and from excruciatingly painful feelings of abandonment. These sufferers seek desperately to escape from that feeling, and are promised to find an escape in yet more 'online'-supplied sex – only to realize that, far from satiating their hunger for human company, this particular internet-cooked and internet-served food only makes its loss more conspicuous and leaves them feeling yet more humiliated, lonely, and famished for warm human togetherness . . .

And there is another issue worth remembering when the gains are balanced against the losses. The online dating agencies (and yet more the instant-sex agencies) tend to introduce the would be partners of one-night stands through a catalogue in which the 'available goods' are classified according to their selected marks, such as height, body type, ethic origin, body hair, etc. (the filing criteria vary depending on the intended public, and its currently dominant ideas of 'relevance'), so that users may patch together their chosen partner out of bits and pieces which they believe to determine the quality of the 'whole' and the pleasures of sex (expecting *their* prospective users to proceed in a similar manner). Somehow in this process the vision of a 'human being' falls apart and vanishes: the forest is no longer seen beyond those trees. Choosing your partner from a catalogue of desirable looks and uses, in the way commodities are chosen from catalogues of online commercial companies, perpetuates the myth which it itself originates and insinuates: that each one of us, human beings, is not so much a person or personality whose unrepeatable worth is all in her or his singularity and uniqueness, but a higgledy-piggledy collection of sellable, or difficult to sell, attributes . . .

7

Strange adventures of privacy (1)

Alain Ehrenberg, a French sociologist and uniquely insightful analyst of the convoluted trajectory of the modern individual, attempted to pinpoint the birthdate of the late modern cultural revolution (at least of its French branch) that ushered us into the times we continue to inhabit; a sort of cultural revolution's equivalent to the first shot of the First World War aimed on 28 June 1914 by Gavrilo Princip at Archduke Franz Ferdinand of Austria and his wife in Sarajevo, or the battleship *Aurora*'s salvo of 7 November 1918, signalling the bolshevik assault and the capture of the Winter Palace. Ehrenberg's choice was an autumnal Wednesday evening in the 1980s when a certain Vivienne declared during a popular TV talk show, and so in front of several million spectators, that her husband Michel's bane of premature ejaculation prevented her from ever experiencing orgasm in the course of her marital life.

What was so revolutionary about Vivienne's pronouncement? Two things. First: a kind of information that until then was deemed to be quintessentially, even eponymously private, was made public. And second: the *public* arena was used to vent and thrash out a matter of thoroughly *private* concern.

What is 'private'? Something that belongs to the realm of 'privacy'. For what is understood by 'privacy', let's consult Wikipedia (the website known to meticulously, and quite often expeditiously seek and swiftly reflect whatever is currently taken by common opinion to be the truth of the matter; and to be zealous in updating it day in, day out, thereby chasing and trying to capture in flight the kinds of targets that are notorious for running faster than even the most dedicated of their pursuers): 'Privacy', I read in the British version of Wikipedia on 8 March 2009,

> is the ability of an individual or group to seclude themselves or information about themselves and thereby reveal themselves selectively . . . Privacy is sometimes related to anonymity, the wish to remain unnoticed or unidentified in the public realm. When something is private to a *person*, it usually means there is something within them that is considered inherently special or personally sensitive . . . Privacy can be seen as an aspect of security – one in which trade-offs between the interests of one group and another can become particularly clear.

And what is the 'public arena'? A space with open access to anyone who wishes to enter. For that reason, everything heard and seen in a 'public arena' may be in principle heard and seen by *anybody*. Those who utter the words and make their moves visible take, and (openly or tacitly, by design or default) accept, the risk of being watched and overheard. They agree to the consequences and abrogate their rights to object or to demand compensation. Considering that (to quote Wikipedia once more) 'the degree to which private information is exposed depends on how the public will receive this information, which differs between places and over time', the effort to keep something private, and the decision to make something public, are obviously at cross-purposes. 'Privacy' and 'publicity' are defined through *opposing* each other.

'Private' and 'public' are at loggerheads. Their semantic fields are not as a rule separated from each other by borders, notoriously inviting/allowing two-way traffic, but by frontlines: impassable boundary lines, preferably tightly sealed and heavily fortified on both sides against trespassers (invaders, but also turncoats, and most particularly deserters). But even if war hasn't been declared, if warlike actions are neither undertaken nor contemplated, and the borderland shows no tendency to turn into a shooting range, borders as a rule tolerate *selected* cross-traffic only. 'Drawing a border' means that the probabilities of specific kinds of traffic are manipulated and intended to be made different (some kinds of traffic to be more, and some less intense) from the way they would otherwise be. Free-for-all traffic would make a mockery out of the very idea of a boundary. Control, and the right to decide who or what is allowed to pass the border and who or what is bound to stay where they are on one side only (what items of information have the prerogative of remaining private, and which ones are allowed or decreed to be made public) – as a rule hotly contested issues – are the reason for drawing a boundary.

For most of the modern era, the assault on the frontier, and yet more importantly any univocal revocation and arbitrary change in the prevailing rules of border traffic, were almost exclusively expected and feared to arrive from the 'public' side: public institutions were widely suspected of an endemic proclivity for snooping and eavesdropping – of an inextinguishable urge to invade and conquer the sphere of the private in order to take it under its own administration, covering it with a dense network of garrisons, spying gadgets and bugging devices, and thereby depriving human individuals or groups of individuals of the shelter offered by a private, untrespassable space; and by the same token, of their personal or group security. Somewhat inconsistently yet not groundlessly all the same, public institutions were suspected of erecting barricades barring access by many a private concern to the agora or other sites of acknowledged mutual communication, where the recasting of private problems into public issues could be negotiated: in other words, of a conspiracy to prohibit certain kind of troubles from being tackled by anybody other than the sufferers themselves.

Obviously, the gruesome experience of communism and Nazism, the two especially rapacious and gory twentieth-century totalitarianisms, lent veracity to such suspicions. Though by now past their peak, those suspicions linger, galvanized time and again by sights or premonitions of public institutions arbitrarily imposing new statutory limits on undertakings previously considered to be left to private discretion, while squeezing out and storing/hiding/locking up for their own (uncontrolled, and therefore potentially harmful) use ever larger amounts of indisputably private, intimate, discretionary information – all that in blatant violation of the usages firmly settled in the democratic mentality even if they were never spelled out and codified.

Whatever the case of the assumed aggressiveness and anticipated rapacity of public institutions led by an all-powerful state,
and however the perception of the state might now be changing,
alerts of that other menace, the one approaching from the opposite
direction, namely the impending invasion and conquest of the
public sphere by what have been seen thus far as exclusively
private affairs, were at best few and far between – if raised and
heard at all; and it was even less frequently that they were listened
to. The task inspiring most of our ancestors and older generations
to be vigilant and take arms was that of defending the private
domain from any undue meddling by the powers that be. People,
gladly or reluctantly, accepted public institutions as their night
watch and bodyguards – but not much more than that. Certainly,
not in their suspected role of obtrusive busybodies peeping through
the thick curtains hanging over people's private affairs.

Until recently, that is . . .

(*to be continued*)

8

Strange adventures of privacy (2)

Peter Sellers, the thoughtful and witty person and exquisite British actor who played dozens of varied and idiosyncratic roles in scores of films, confessed: 'If you asked me to play myself, I would not know what to do. I do not know who or what I am.' He added, pensively, 'There used to be a me behind the mask, but I had it surgically removed.' William Shakespeare, while prophetically and insightfully anticipating Sellers' query, went a step still further and asked through King Lear's lips: 'Who is it that can tell me who I am?'

Except in the case of so-called 'rhetorical questions' that tend to pre-empt the answer and/or imply that the answers are foregone conclusions, an act of asking normally presumes or signals that the issue is moot. Indeed, as each of us has learned (even if in a way somewhat less tragic and painful than Lear's), it is not just up to me to say who or what I am. In my disagreement and continuous litigation with others around me as to 'who or what I am', many voices – often sharply dissonant – are heard. Who in all that tussle currently sits in judgement and has the power to decide and impose an outcome is anything but clear. Just how much leeway will others offer me in painting my own image for, so to speak, 'public consumption' (an image I'd consider to be my true likeness with others agreeing, even if reluctantly, with my opinion) is an issue unlikely ever to be ultimately, irrevocably settled. Any settlement is unlikely to be the last. In all probability, each will remain open to reassessment and renegotiation – and permanently . . .

On secrecy (and so obliquely on privacy, individuality, autonomy, self-definition and self-assertion, for the simple reason that the right to secrecy is an indispensable, crucial, defining attribute of them all), Georg Simmel, arguably the most insightful of the founders of sociology, commented that to stand a realistic chance of survival, the right to keep secrets needs to be acknowledged by others. Simmel suggests that secrecy, while being an integral part of privacy, is also a *social relation*: a rule, he insists, needs to be observed that 'what is intentionally or unintentionally *hidden* is intentionally or unintentionally *respected*' (italics added). The relation between these two conditions (of privacy, and of the social recognition/tolerance/protection of individual autonomy) tends to be unstable and tense, however – and for that reason 'the intention of hiding' 'takes on a much greater intensity when it clashes with the intention of revealing'. If that 'greater intensity' fails to emerge, if the urge to defend secrecy tooth and nail against interlopers, meddlers and busybodies disrespectful of one's secrets is absent, or not followed through diligently enough, privacy is in danger.

Something secret, by definition, is that part of one's knowledge which one refuses to share with others. Secrecy, the protection of information from being divulged without due authorization, draws, marks and fortifies the boundaries of privacy; and privacy is the realm that is meant to be one's kingdom, the land of one's sole and indivisible sovereignty, inside which one has full power to decide 'what and who I am', and from which one may launch and relaunch at will campaigns to have one's own decisions duly recognized and respected. In my last letter, I wrote, however, that 'defending the private domain from any undue meddling by the powers that be' was the sole task inspiring most of our ancestors and older generations to take arms – but added right away: until quite recently . . .

In a startling U-turn from the habits of our ancestors, we've somehow lost a considerable part of the guts, the stamina, and the will to persist in the defence of that 'private domain'. In our days, it is not so much the possibility of betrayal or violation of privacy that frightens us but its opposite: shutting down the exits from the private world, turning the private domain into a site of incarceration, a solitary confinement cell, or even a dungeon of the kind into which people who fell from favour with the ruler in bygone times used to disappear amid a void of public unconcern and oblivion – the owner of that 'private space' being sentenced to stew forever in his or her own juice. The absence of avid listeners eager to wring, tear, squeeze or steal our secrets from behind the ramparts of privacy, to put them on public display and make them everybody's property, and prompting everybody to wish to share them, is perhaps the most nightmarish of nightmares tormenting our contemporaries. 'Being a celebrity' (that is, constantly on public view, having neither a need for nor the right to secrecy) is today the most obtrusively popularized and most popular model of successful life.

More and more of our fellow human beings are inclined to believe (even if they would not say this in so many words) that there is no joy in having secrets – except the kinds of secrets meant and fit to be joyously disclosed in order to be displayed on the internet, on TV, on the front pages of tabloids and on the covers of glossy magazines. As a result, it is now the *public* sphere that finds itself flooded and overwhelmed, having been invaded by the troops of *privacy*. But are those new invading troops rushing to conquer new outposts and spawn new garrisons, or are they rather escaping the enclosures where they feel they are suffocating; running away, in despair and panic, from past shelters, now no longer habitable? Are their assaults symptoms of a newly acquired spirit of exploration and conquest – or rather testimonies to expropriation, victimization, and eviction orders? Is the task they have been ordered to perform – the task of finding out and/or deciding 'what and who I am' – too daunting to be seriously undertaken in the confines of the skimpy plot of privacy? But can that task (contrary to what Peter Sellers found) be fulfilled by being performed on the public stage, with means publicly recommended and supplied: such as trial-and-error testing of many tentative approaches, or the putting on and taking off of many different dresses? Or is it rather the other way round: the more zealously one deploys such means, the less likely the prospect becomes of reaching the desired result – that certainty one is after and hopes to acquire?

These are only some of the questions with no obvious, straightforward, indisputable, let alone irrefutable answers. There is, however, another set of crucial questions, similarly waiting for a convincing answer, thus far in vain. Secrecy, after all, is not only a tool of privacy, for cutting out a space entirely of one's own, for setting oneself apart from intruders and uncomfortable and thus unwelcome companions; it is also a powerful tool of *togetherness*, for tying together arguably the strongest of known and conceivable *interhuman bonds*. By confiding one's secrets to some selected, few, 'very special' people, while barring them to all the others, the webs of friendship are woven, one's 'best friends' are appointed and retained, unconditional and permanent commitments are entered into and maintained, and loose aggregates of individuals are magically transformed into tightly knit and integrated groups. In short, enclaves are cut out of the world inside which the troublesome and vexing clash between belonging and autonomy is, for once, laid to rest; in these enclaves the choices between private interest and the well-being of others, between altruism and selfishness, self-love and the care of another, stop being tormenting and no longer foment and fan pangs of conscience.

But, as Thomas Szasz observed (in *The Second Sin*) as early as 1973, 'traditionally, sex has been a very private, secretive activity. Herein perhaps lies its powerful force for uniting people in a strong bond. As we make sex less secretive, we may rob it of its power to hold men and women together.' Szasz put sex under his microscope because sexual pursuits served until recently as the most drastic example, indeed a genuine epitome, of an intimate secret meant to be shared with the utmost discretion, solely with the most carefully and laboriously selected others; in other words, as the strongest, most difficult to break, most reliable variety of interhuman bonds. But what applies to what was until recently the most prominent object and most effective guardian of privacy applies even more to its lesser companions, inferior substitutes and paler copies. The present-day crisis of privacy seems to be, in other words, inextricably connected with the weakening, the disintegration and the decay of all and any interhuman bonds. In this process, one tendency is an egg and the other a chicken, and as in all similar cases, it is waste of time to quarrel which came first and which comes second . . .

(*to be continued*)

9
Strange adventures of privacy (3)

Technological innovations are too often blamed or praised for causing cultural revolutions; they manage at most to trigger them, by supplying a final link missing in an otherwise complete chain of factors needed to shift a transformation in prevailing lifestyles and mores from the realm of possibility into that of reality: a transformation long ready and desperately struggling to happen. One of such technological innovations is the mobile/cellular telephone.

The advent of the mobile made the state of being constantly at people's beck and call feasible; indeed, a realistic postulate and expectation, and a demand difficult to refuse for its fulfilment have been – for tough objective reasons – assumed impossible. By the same token, the entry of the mobile into social life effaced, for all practical intents and purposes, the borderline between private and public time, private and public space, workplace and home, work-time and leisure time, 'here' and 'there' (the owner of a mobile-phone number being constantly and everywhere 'here', that is within reach). Or, at least, it has stripped all such borderlines of much of their power to hold and arrest, making their effacement or trespassing over an easy and plausible accomplishment – at any rate technically. 'Being away' does not, has not and should not now be tantamount to 'being out of reach'. One can still, to be sure, leave the mobile on the table before going out, misplace it or just be unable to find it in time – but all such explanations of failure to respond to a ringing call for attention can now be viewed as evidence of negligence, insubordination, condemnable and offensive indifference, a snub – and innumerable other, but similarly personal and subjective faults or ill intentions. Mobile phones are the technical foundation of *the presumption of constant accessibility and availability*. A presumption that the human condition common in our liquid modern setting, the condition of 'loners being constantly in touch', has already been made feasible, and indeed turned into a 'norm' – in the second of its two aspects as much as in the first.

If applied selectively, 'constant availability' can be, and indeed is, widely nowadays used to organize the public space: to divide it into areas of 'connectivity' and 'non-connectivity'. Everyone *can* be constantly available now, but one still needs to *make* oneself available – and one does, though *to selected others* only. Making oneself available is a tool of network-building: simultaneously of unification and separation, of 'coming into touch' and 'keeping out of touch'. Inclusion in the network, marked by exchanging mobile numbers, presumes a reciprocal promise to be 'always there for you', and an obligation to resort to that always-keen-and-ready presence (though of course, like all other patterns and stratagems of reciprocation, this one can be and often is, contrary to overt presumptions, abused for unilateral exploitation, to the discomfort and irritation of the alleged or assumed partner). Mobile phones are the building blocks of mini public footholds, spaces in which a mini-version of the status of celebrity, known and seen to be displayed in truly and fully 'public' expanses, can be fought for, experimented with, and enjoyed by all the rest of us . . .

Mobile numbers (that is, the address of the mobile-mediated 'here' where one can always be found, ready to respond and interact) are not listed in telephone directories, and thereby not accessible to every Tom, Dick or Harry; offering one's mobile phone number is for that reason an act of bestowing and/or applying for a distinction: an act of admission coupled with consent, and/or a request, to be admitted. That practice is now shaping our image of the 'network' – the vision of togetherness that came to replace the concept of the 'group', and particularly of the 'community of belonging'. It has become, indeed, the archetype of the current rendition of an evergreen private/public issue.

From among such images of the forms of togetherness it has elbowed out or replaced altogether, the concept of 'network' stands out most prominently by its flexibility, and by its deceptive amenability to close monitoring and management as well as to swift and painless adjustment and refurbishment. It is also distinguished by its unique portability: unlike other collections of people, 'networks' as recorded in the owners' handsets follow them, in the manner of a snail's home, wherever they may move or stop at any moment. It therefore offers its owner an illusion of 'being in control', permanently and continuously.

A network has, even if in a miniaturized form, all the markings of a public space, yet its size and content are cut to the owner's individual predilections and preferences, staying easy to cleanse through the simple act of pressing the 'delete' key, obliterating the parts that no longer match the owner's expectations or arouse the owner's interest; for those reasons it appears (and from time to time also feels) as if it is docilely submissive and responsive to the owner's changing moods and wishes. The frailty of connections, the instant accessibility of the facilities for disconnecting, in short a coupling of an easiness of getting in touch with the painlessness of instantaneously terminating the condition of 'being in touch' at the moment it turns constraining and inconvenient – all these seem to be eminently geared to the capricious dialectics of convoluted private and public relationships. They seem to open quite new and wider vistas to individual freedom, while disabling the snares of commitment scattered all over the public realm. And yet . . .

As José Saramago puts it (in *O homem duplicado* (*The Double*), 2002, here quoted in Margaret Jull Costa's translation), in his inimitably perceptive and poignant manner: 'Why it is that while communication technologies continue to develop in a genuinely geometric progression, from improvement to improvement, the other form of communication, proper, real communication, from me to you, from us to them, should still be this confusion crisscrossed with cul-de-sacs, so deceiving with its illusory esplanades, as devious in expression as in concealment' . . . The 'perplexity when faced by the genuine Cretan labyrinth of human relationships', so Saramago concludes and suggests, is 'incurable'. Perplexity is here to stay, even if communication technologies go on developing in a geometrical, even in exponential, progression.

As I'd add to Saramago's observation, that perplexity is, if anything, likely to grow. The greatest achievement of the communication technologies in question has not been, after all, the simplification of the infuriatingly complex practice of human cohabitation, but its compressing into a thin and shallow layer amenable, unlike the multilayered, thick and dense original, to simplification thanks to its ability to be unproblematically and effortlessly handled. The side-effect of this removal of 'proper, real communication' (as Saramago chooses to call the pristine, uncompressed version) from the agenda of urgent tasks, not to be put aside, is a further wilting, fading and vanishing of the skills which such 'proper, real communication' necessarily requires.

The ultimate result of all that is that the challenges of the 'from me to you, from us to them' communication look yet more daunting and confusing, and the art of handling them effectively appears even more nebulous and difficult to master than it did before the start of that 'greatest revolution in human connectedness' (as the invention and entrenchment of mobile phones has been baptised).

10
Parents and children

In a film, *Le diable, probablement*, released by Robert Bresson in 1977, an era with no inkling as yet of PCs, mobile phones, iPods and other wonders of socializing/separating, contacting/isolating, connecting/disconnecting technology, the heroes are several youths who are clearly at a loss as they desperately seek a purpose in life, their assignments in the world and the meaning of their 'being assigned'. No help was there for them from their elders. As a matter of fact, not a single adult appeared on screen in the 95 minutes needed by the plot to reach its tragic denouement. Only once in all that time was the sheer existence of adults noticed by the youngsters, fully absorbed as they were in the vexingly abortive effort to communicate with each other: when the youngsters, tired out by their exploits, felt hungry and gathered around a fridge stuffed with food stored for such an occasion by their otherwise unnoticed and all but invisible parents. Just how prophetic Bresson's cinematic vision was, the three decades that followed its release disclosed and convincingly confirmed. Bresson saw through to the consequences of the 'great transformation' he and his contemporaries were witnessing, though only a few of them had the perspicacity to note them, the wisdom to scrutinize them and the passion to record them: the passage from a society of producers – workers and soldiers – to a society of consumers – individuals through and through and, as decreed by their historical location, devotees of short-term thoughts, perspectives and undertakings.

The parental role in the preceding, 'solid modern' society of producers and soldiers consisted of instilling in their offspring, by hook or by crook, the lifelong self-discipline needed to endure the monotonous routine of an industrial workplace or a military barracks – while serving as personal role models for their children of such 'normatively regulated' behaviour. Michel Foucault took the case of infantile sexuality and the 'masturbation panic' of the nineteenth and twentieth centuries as a specimen of the well-stocked arsenal of weapons, to be deployed in the legitimation and promotion of strict control and full-time surveillance, which parents of that era were expected to exercise over their children.[4] This sort of parental role

> demanded constant, attentive, and curious presences for its exercise; it presupposed proximities; it proceeded through examination and insistent observation; it required an exchange of discourses, through questions that extorted admissions, and confidences that went beyond the questions that were asked. It implied a physical proximity and an interplay of intense sensations.

Foucault suggested that in that perpetual campaign to strengthen the parental role and its disciplining impact 'the child's "vice" was not so much an enemy as a support': 'Wherever there was a chance that [vice] might appear, devices of surveillance were installed; traps were laid for compelling admissions.' Bathrooms and bedrooms were stigmatized as the sites of the greatest danger, the most fertile plantations for children's morbid sexual inclinations – and so those sites called for particularly close, intimate, unrelenting supervision, and of course for a constantly watchful and interfering, obtrusive parental presence.

In our liquid modern times, masturbation has been absolved from its supposed sins – while the masturbation panic has been replaced by the 'sexual abuse' panic. The hidden menace, the cause of the new panic, has not, however, been located in the children's, but in their parents' sexuality. Bathroom and bedrooms are, as before, seen as dens of gruesome vice, but it is now the *parents* (and adults in general, all of them suspected of being potential child molesters and abusers) who stand accused of being its carriers. Whether openly declared and manifest, or latent and tacit, the ends pursued by the war declared on the newly noticed and currently fought villains are a slackening of parental control, a renunciation of the parents' ubiquitous and obtrusive presence in their children's lives, a setting and maintaining of a distance between the 'old' and the 'young' – both inside the family and in the circle of family friends.

As to the present panic, the latest report by l'Institut National de la Démographie shows that in the six years from 2000 to 2006 the number of men and women interviewed recalling cases of sexual abuse in their childhood almost tripled (from 2.7 per cent to 7.3 per cent – to 16 per cent of the women and 5 per cent of the men – with the trend, if anything, fast accelerating).[5] The authors of the report underline that 'the rise does not prove the growing incidence of aggression, but a growing inclination to report rape events in scientific surveys, reflecting the lowering of the threshold of tolerance of violence' – but it is tempting to add that it reflects as well, and perhaps to an even higher degree, the rising, media-insinuated tendency to explain current adult psychological afflictions and problems by their presumed or imputed childhood experiences of sexual harassment and abuse, rather than by frustrated childhood sexuality and the Oedipus or Electra complexes. Let us be clear that the issue is not how many parents, with or without the complicity of other adults, do in fact treat their children as sexual objects, and to what extent they abuse their superior powers to profit from children's weakness – just as in the past the issue was not how many of their children surrendered to their masturbating urges; what *does* matter, and matters gravely and seminally, is that all of them have been loudly and publicly warned that narrowing the distance which they are instructed to keep between themselves, and other adults, and their children may be (must be and will be) interpreted as releasing – overtly, surreptitiously or subconsciously – their endemic paedophiliac urges.

The prime casualty of the masturbation panic was the *autonomy of the young*. Starting from their early childhood, would-be adults were to be protected against their own morbid and potentially disastrous (if left uncontrolled) instincts and impulses. The prime casualties of the sexual abuse panic are instead bound to be *intergenerational bonds and intimacy*. If the masturbation panic cast the adult as a best friend, guardian angel, trusted guide and all in all an indispensable warden of the young, the panic about sexual abuse casts adults as the 'usual suspects', charged a priori with crimes he or she must have intended to commit, or at least been driven to commit instinctively, with or without malice aforethought. The first panic resulted in a sharp increase of parental power, but it also induced the adults to acknowledge their responsibility to and for the young, and to diligently perform the duties which followed from it. The new panic releases the adults, for a change, from their duties – by presenting them a priori as the agents responsible for actual or potential abuse of power.

This new panic adds a legitimizing gloss to an already advanced process of the *commercialization of the parent–child relationship* – by forcefully mediating this relationship through the consumer market. Whatever remnants of moral scruples may linger following the retreat of the parents from their watchful and caring presence in the family home, consumer markets propose to stifle through transforming every family feast or religious and national holiday into an occasion to lavish on their children costly dream-gifts, and through aiding and abetting, day after day, the flourishing one-upmanship of children, manoeuvred as they are in a fierce competition with their peers into displaying shop-supplied tokens of social distinction.

Resort to the help of such an alluring consumer industry may, however, be a means of 'buying oneself out of trouble' that creates more problems than it manages to resolve. Professor Frank Furedi noted the resulting 'deskilling' of adults in their task of exercising adult authority: 'If adults are not trusted to be near children,' he asks, 'is it any surprise that at least some of them draw the conclusion that they are really not expected to take responsibility for the well-being of children in their community?'[6]

11

Teenager spending

The Office for National Statistics has published its latest 'household spending survey' for the UK, reporting on the current structure of an average family's budget: for what purposes money is spent by people living together under one roof, what it is spent on, and by whom. The report shows that an 'average teenager' in Britain spends more than £1,000 a year on mobile phones, MP3 players and downloads, £240 on haircuts and £300 on trainers. These are not the only regular items of expenditures: to arrive at the whole teenage budget, money needs to be added for cinemas, clubbing and clothes. There is also the 'must have' gear which the average teenager considers to be absolutely necessary for a decent, indeed 'normal' life and to be accepted into the company of his or her age-mates and respected by them: things like mobile phones, duly upgraded to a 'new and improved' version and regularly fed with updated ringtones; a laptop; a TV and DVD player in their own room; some musical instrument(s) and music lessons . . . All in all, the average teenager's lifestyle, according to the survey, costs £9,000 a year. Corrected for inflation, this means 12 times more than the average teenager used to spend around 30 years ago.

There are two more points to consider before we digest those figures and take a stand. The first point: the teenage kind of spending starts much earlier now than it did when the statistical calculations began – and the starting point continues to move down the age scale. For instance, one of the educational charities found in a recent study that seven-year-olds wish to possess not just their own mobiles, but also the currently fashionable ringtones and the most recently advertised games to go with them.

And the second point: teenagers of the 1970s were, much like their present-day successors, cajoled, tempted and seduced to enjoy the wonders of console games, portable music players or cinema outings; but all such objects of desire (perhaps with the exception of cinema tickets) were (relatively) much more expensive then and so less accessible than the much more sophisticated versions of today. Those objects of desire were seen as luxuries, objects of dreams rather than needs – and their possession was viewed as a stroke of a particularly kind and generous, selectively benevolent luck, not a legitimate expectation and certainly not a matter of right or duty. Now that each of the desired items is cheaper, falling temptingly downwards in price and so coming seductively within reach, their acquisition tends to become a routine part of ordinary, 'normal', 'everybody who is anybody' life – no longer a one-off, extraordinary event to celebrate and memorize, to thank God or good fortune for and write home about. The unexpected, yet inescapable effect is that the emotional bond with the acquired items is all but gone: it is the *moment of acquisition* that really counts – not the *lasting friendship*. Half of all mobiles possessed by teenagers end up being lost or just misplaced, and trainers, no longer sought and coveted, end up in the rubbish bin soon after being bought. Things fall out of fashion as rapidly as they burst into it. In the stream of chattels quickly acquired and fast abandoned and disposed of, hardly anything stands out as 'a proud possession dear to the heart,' – and if it does, then surely not for long. It is the *style* that needs to be kept forever alive, not its *paraphernalia* – and that style requires that its accessories succeed one another at an ever accelerating pace.

It was Giacomo Segantini, one of my Italian readers, whose thoughtful letter prompted me to visit the world of teenagers once more. He wrote: 'The reality which I live personally is completely different. I consume as little as possible, as I don't have money to do otherwise. This circumstance, rather than causing frustration, has accustomed me to ignoring marketing messages.' I have no reason to doubt my correspondent's sincerity, and can only admire the strength of his will, however much its strength might have been beefed up by the pressure of necessity. Giacomo Segantini chose or was forced to swim against the current – and a powerful one. There are many other young men and women who just like him 'don't have money' for the kind of lifestyle widely believed to be a matter of (social) life or (social) death. There are many regarded as 'insufficient' or 'inadequate', flawed or failed consumers – yet that condition hardly made them happy; they wouldn't choose it if they had the choice. 'Marketing messages' are ubiquitous, obtrusively insistent and insidious, though their most awesome power derives from the fact that most of their addressees' age-mates ('average teenagers') listen to them with awe, and try as well as they can (and more than they can) to follow their instructions and commands. So it is not just the pressure of the commercials, but also, and probably more than anything else, the less obtrusive perhaps, yet most certainly powerfully effective pressure of the people around, of the standards they struggle to match and expect all others in their company to match, that one has to get accustomed 'to ignoring'. And ignoring, playing down, overcoming social pressure takes courage – a lot of courage. It calls for nerves of steel – and a strong character; very strong indeed, not easy to train, to cultivate, to preserve through thick and thin.

If 30 years ago it took some special, selected people, particularly determined and outstandingly brave, to patiently save money for a personal computer, or for the privilege of watching films by the directors they admired and/or featuring the actors they adored – in recent years it has taken special people, particularly determined and blessed with an outstanding power of resistance, to refuse to go into debt for the sake of purchasing right away the latest MP3 player and downloading the latest tunes. Giacomo Segantini could have been one of that special and not very numerous breed, and I guess that being a special person did not come to him easily; he must often have found it painful, and on more than one occasion also humiliating . . . Surrendering to the tide has a monetary price. Swimming against it has its price as well; not monetary in this case, but often bringing more hurt and being more difficult to pay. In one of my letters I wrote that fate sets the options, but character makes the choices. Judging from Segantini's choices, there is every reason to admire and respect his character.

I was also impressed by Giacomo's insistence that it is impossible 'not to think about future'. Considering the date of his letter (a few months after the recent credit collapse, and the following collapse of labour markets) it seems that, this time, Giacomo is rejoining the ranks of a large majority of his age-mates. It looks as if the kind of life spent among the vertiginous, exhilarating and breathtaking whirl of novel goods and excitements that not so long ago was expected to continue forever is now grinding to a halt – at any rate its pace is slowing down, and it seems likely to go on limping for some time yet. As Giacomo Segantini rightly writes, 'not dozens, but hundreds of thousands' of young people entering the adult world together with him are facing up to a challenge of a kind of which half a year ago they had no inkling, and certainly did not have the skill to confront. They were trained to deal and cope with an *excess* of options and opportunities; instead they need to learn, and fast, how to live in a world afflicted by their *dearth*. Is there a job waiting for me? If so, what kind of a job? What must I do to get it? You can name a few possible jobs, yet neither you nor I can vouch that they are still around, and will stay around long enough for us to acquire the skills they demand.

I would be delighted were Giacomo to succeed in joining, as he mentions, the ranks of 'young sociologists', though I must warn him (and everybody contemplating a similar choice) that joining those particular ranks won't make his life easier. Given his character, it may on the contrary add to his worries and further detract from whatever is left of his spiritual comfort. Because as a sociologist, he will find out again and again, repeatedly throughout his professional life, that 'men learn only what would be of use to their grandparents. The right way to live is something we can teach only the dead' – as Fernando Pessoa, believed by many to be the author 'of one of the defining texts of the modern world', once observed.

12

Stalking the Y generation

No human being is exactly like another – and this observation applies to the young as much as to the old. All the same, it is possible to note that in a certain category of human beings some traits or qualities tend to appear more frequently than in the rest. It is this 'relative condensation' of features that allows us to speak of 'categories' in the first place: be it nations, classes, genders – or generations. When we do, we close our eyes for a time to the multitude of characteristics that make each member of the 'category' into a unique, unrepeatable entity, unlike any other, a being standing out from all the other members of 'the same category' – and focus instead on features that are common to all or most category members in contrast to their absence or relative rarity among the members of other 'categories'. It is with this proviso constantly in mind that we are allowed to talk of all our contemporaries, except the eldest among us, as 'belonging' to three successive generations.

The first is the 'Boomers' generation: people born between 1946 and 1964, during the notorious postwar 'baby boom', when the soldiers returning from battlefronts and prisoner-of-war camps decided that the time had arrived to plan for the future, to marry and to bring children into the world. Still fresh in the heads and hearts of the returning soldiers were the prewar years of unemployment, scarcity and austerity, a hand-to-mouth existence with a threat of destitution it was impossible to thwart or hold at a safe distance from the doorstep; no wonder that having returned home from the battlefields they gladly embraced the offers of employment that were suddenly and uncharacteristically abundant, though, with the wisdom of their earlier bitter experiences, they welcomed them as a gift of good fortune that could at any moment be withdrawn. For that reason they worked long and hard, saving pennies for a rainy day and to give their children a chance of the trouble-free life they themselves never savoured.

Their children, 'Generation X', now aged between 28 and 45, were born into a different world; the world their parents' dedication, long working hours, prudence, parsimony and self-denial helped to bring about. Though they practised the life philosophy and strategy of their parents, they adopted it rather reluctantly – increasingly impatient, as the world around grew richer and life prospects more secure, to see and enjoy the rewards of their parents' and particularly their own temperance, moderation and self-denial. They worried about the future less than their parents, concerning themselves more with the 'now': with the life pleasures within reach, ready to consume on the spot. This is why they have been often dubbed, pungently yet poignantly, a 'me generation' . . .

And then 'Generation Y' arrived, now aged between 11 and 28. As numerous observers and researchers agree, it differs sharply from the generations of their parents and grandparents. They were born into a world their parents did not know in their early youth and which they would have found difficult, if not downright impossible, to imagine then, and would greet with a mixture of bafflement and distrust when it arrived in their later life: a world of abundant employment, seemingly infinite choices, plentiful opportunities to be enjoyed, each more alluring than others – and of being able to multiply pleasures to taste, each more seductive than the others and each pushing its predecessor into early retirement and ultimate oblivion.

What is constantly, abundantly and matter-of-factly within reach tends to 'hide in the light' – it is too obvious to be noticed, let alone pondered on. Without air to breathe you wouldn't survive more than a minute or two, but were you asked to make a list of things you consider to be your 'life necessities', air would hardly crop up in it; while in the unlikely event it did, it would appear very far down. You just assume, without thinking, that air is there,

anytime and everywhere, and that you need do next to nothing to
ingest as much of it as your lungs fancy. Until a year or so ago,
work (in our part of the world at least) was in this respect like
air: always available whenever you needed it – and if it happened
to be lacking for a moment (like fresh air in a crowded room), a
minimum of effort (such as opening a window) would have suf-
ficed to bring things 'back to normal'. However amazing this
might have seemed to members of the 'Boomer' or even the 'X'
generation, it was no wonder that, according to numerous researchers, 'work' fell close to the bottom of the lists of 'items indispensable to a good life' that members of Generation Y tended to
compose. If pressed to justify this neglect, they would answer:
'Work? It is, alas, indispensable [again, like air] to staying alive.
But on its own it would not make life worth living – rather the
opposite: it may make it dull, dreary and unappetizing because
monotonous. Work may prove to be a chore and a bore – nothing
interesting happening, nothing to catch your imagination, nothing
to stimulate your senses. If a job gives you little pleasure, at any
rate it should not stand in the way of things that truly matter!'
What were they, the things that truly mattered? A lot of free time
outside the office, shop or factory, time off work whenever something more interesting cropped up elsewhere, travelling, being in
the places and among the friends of your choice – all those things
having one feature in common: they all tend to occur outside the
workplace. Life is elsewhere! Whatever life-project members of
Generation Y might entertain, cherish and apply themselves to
was unlikely to be wrapped around employment – let alone around
a steady job from here to eternity. The last thing they would
appreciate in work would be its long-term stability, with a prospect of infinity . . .

Research shows that when they looked for young talent, the
most reputable recruiting agencies were fully aware of Generation's Y's priorities and phobias. They were at pains to focus their
seductive recruitment campaigns on the freedom the offered
employment promised to guarantee: flexible working hours,
working from home, sabbaticals, long leaves with the job retained
for the duration – and entertaining and relaxing opportunities in
office time and inside the workplace. The agencies accepted that
if the newcomers found the work uninteresting, they would simply
quit and move elsewhere. Since the prospect of unemployment,

that cruel, inhuman, but most effective guardian of workforce stability, was for a considerable time no longer frightening, there was little else to stop them doing just that.

Well, if this is the kind of life philosophy and life strategy that used to distinguish Generation Y from its predecessors, the young people of the present are due for a rude awakening. The most prosperous countries of Europe expect mass and protracted unemployment to return from oblivion and from its allegedly permanent exile. If that dark premonition materializes, the infinite choice and freedom of movement and change which the contemporary young came to view (or, rather, were born to see) as part of nature are about to disappear – together with the ostensibly unlimited credit they hoped would sustain them in the event of (temporary and brief) adversity, and see them through the (temporary and brief) lack of an immediate and satisfactory solution to their troubles.

To the members of Generation Y, this may come as a shock. Unlike the Boomer Generation, they have no 'second line of trenches' – no old memories and half-forgotten skills, no store of tricks, once tried but long unused, to fall back on. A world of harsh, non-negotiable realities, of scarcity and enforced austerity, of times of trouble when 'quitting' is no solution is, for a great many of them, a totally foreign country; a country they have never visited – and if they have, it was one they would never have seriously considered settling in; a country so mysterious that it would require a long and hard, not at all pleasant, apprenticeship to accommodate.

It remains to be seen in what shape Generation Y will be when it emerges from this test. And what life philosophy the Generation Z about to follow it will design, embrace and deploy to refurbish the world inherited from their fathers . . .

13

Freedom's false dawn

Not that long ago Siobhan Healey, now 23 years young, acquired her first credit card. She welcomed it as the dawn of her freedom, to be remembered and celebrated year in, year out, as the day of liberation. From that day on, she was her own master, free to manage her own finances, free to choose her own priorities and to match her realities with her desires.

Not long after that day Siobhan acquired a second credit card – to service the debt she incurred on the first. Not long after that, she also learned the price to be paid for her cherished 'financial freedom' – as soon as she found that the second card wouldn't suffice to pay the interest on the debt accumulated on the first. She turned to a bank for a loan to pay the arrears on both cards, which by then had reached the terrifying heights of 26,000 Australian dollars. But, following the example of her friends – a 'must' for everyone of her age – she borrowed yet more to finance her overseas travel. Shortly after, it finally dawned upon her that there was little chance of ever getting clear on her own: that taking more loans is not a way to repay your debts. She said, alas a year or two too late: 'I have had to completely change my thought pattern and learn to "save to buy".' And she employed a financial counsellor and visited a debt agreement administrator to help her wriggle and crawl her way out of debt. But would they help her 'to completely change' her 'thought pattern'? That remains to be seen, but the odds are that Siobhan will face an uphill struggle . . .

Ben Paris, a spokesman for Debt Mediators Australia, was neither surprised nor baffled by Siobhan's trials and tribulations. He compared her story to 'shuffling deck chairs on the Titanic', but added immediately that young people 'borrow way beyond their means'. And he pointed out that the case of Siobhan Healey was in no way exceptional: 'We talk to 25,000 young people a year who are in financial distress – and we're just seeing the tip of the iceberg.'

Is Siobhan Healey, and the thousands of other young people in a similar predicament, to be disparaged and condemned for her reckless and myopic conduct? There are more than enough reasons for her to be. But when you rush to denounce her thoughtlessness, don't forget that there are people much older, more experienced and soberly calculating who – to say the least – have their own share in the guilt. Lending companies live on and profit from borrowers; people who refuse to borrow and resist living on credit are of no use to them; people willing to borrow heavily, indeed to borrow 'beyond their means', are, on the contrary, wholeheartedly welcomed by them: they are, after all, the kind of people most likely to be constant sources of profit through remaining interest-payers from here to eternity . . . No wonder that lending companies and bank and credit card managers do whatever promises to be most effective in drawing as many people as possible into the borrowing game, rightly hoping that once in the game, borrowers won't easily find salvation in anything except borrowing yet more . . .

And what is the most propitious time for the transformation of the 'saving to buy' kind of people into debtors-for-life? The moment when they are at their most vulnerable, the moment of transition from childhood to adulthood, when childhood habits still linger, even while they turn ever more inadequate in the face of the novel allurements, demands and challenges of adult existence. A child is, and rightly, used to things coming as gifts, with no strings attached . . . Money tends to be given not in order to be repossessed with interest, but out of parental love and care. As a token of love, not greed. Questions such as 'will you be able to repay me?' are never asked, collateral is never demanded, a date of repayment (if any) is never fixed. If a child asks Mum or Dad for a few coins or even banknotes on the top of their weekly allowance of pocket money, the response will be 'what do you need it for?', not 'do you have enough property of your own as collateral?' Parents will give or deny another gift depending on their son's or daughter's urgency of needs or intensity of desire – not on their ability to repay. Most parents assume without pondering that their children will repay their lavish gifts with the gifts they will in time lavish on their grandchildren . . . This is how the world rolls on, isn't it?

Eventually, and inevitably, a time arrives, however, when young people, no longer children but not yet adults either, will wish to settle on their own. To manage their own affairs. To decide on their own where to move and what to do and what their priorities are. And a time arrives when parents, even the most loving and caring parents (not out of selfishness, but because of their love and care) will expect their sons and daughters to 'become somebody' – work and earn their living. And a time arrives when sons and daughters (not out of resentment, but because of their gratitude and love for their parents) dearly wish to oblige: to prove that they are indeed able to live up to their dad's and mum's expectations.

For lending companies, this is a wonderful time to strike, and to hit a bull's eye. The parents' place in the world map carried in the heads of young adults is suddenly vacant; for moneylenders, that signals a never-to-be-repeated occasion to slip *in loco parentis*. Just like the wolf in the tale of Red Riding Hood, trying to stand in for her sweet old grandma – only hoping that this time round sweet little Red Riding Hood won't be as insightful and clever as in the fairytale original, and so won't call their bluff in time; or that she won't notice the bluff at all because now the descendants of Red Riding Hood do not wander alone in the woods, but come in crowds, and in a crowd each one tends, unthinkingly, to behave like everyone else rather than accept the drudgery and risks of thinking for themselves.

What makes the lot of youngsters still more difficult to avoid is the fact that in many countries lending companies gain powerful support from state governments that introduce theoretical, but also practical courses in the 'art of living on credit' into the obligatory curriculum of all colleges and universities, whatever faculty and degree has been chosen. Loans, unavoidable when studying for a degree, have been made – with the help of a rising number of governments – to be seductively yet misleadingly easy to obtain, and to appear seductively yet deceptively easy to repay. As a result, an average student finishes her or his study with a debt which many graduates will sooner or later find much too huge ever to be repaid in full; a debt which almost guarantees that more debts will be required to be entered into in order to service it . . . The pump of a life-on-credit having been thereby primed, from now on the taking on of new loans to repay the old will look like nothing more than just following a normal routine. A vicious circle indeed. Such circles can't be untied – only cut.

This letter started as a sailor's story, but fast turned into a peasant's one (if you still remember the difference, explained in the first of my letters . . .). How many replicas of Siobhan Healey have moved into your neighbourhood? Perhaps into your home? Your bed? Your pyjamas?

14

The arrival of child-women

As we learn from Diana Appleyard on dailymail.co.uk, Georgie Swann reads two weekly fashion magazines every week and 'spends a lot of time in her bedroom trying on her favourite outfits and her large collection of shoes and handbags'. She adores make-up and keeps in her room about 20 lip glosses. At the time of Diana Appleyard's description, Georgie was saving money for a breast implant and could hardly wait for it to be done, dreaming about being more like the model Jordan, her idol. Well, you might say that there are many women like Georgie, that there is nothing particularly new about that piece of news – if it were not for the fact that Georgie was . . . ten years old.

Appleyard suggests that Georgie is just one example of a growing category of what she calls 'child women'. She quotes a longitudinal study into childhood in the UK, conducted by Bob Reitemeier, the chief executive of the Children's Society, which shows that fewer than 20 per cent of children regularly play outside, while the majority of ten-year-old girls 'are obsessed by hair, fashion and make-up', and 26 per cent feel they are not thin enough and are obsessed with their weight. Reitemeier noted with alarm the fast rise in levels of anxiety among young girls, who feel that 'they are not thin enough, not beautiful enough, and compare themselves to the impossible images of their airbrushed idols in magazines'.

Georgie's parents approved of and enjoyed their ten-year-old daughter's habits, considering them 'harmless and fun'. But

Appleyard's report prompted 271 readers to comment, and most of them were amazed and piqued by what they had read, condemning Georgie's 'premature maturation' and blaming her parents as the ones responsible for her faults: first, by being unforgivably inattentive, lenient and indulgent; second, by being 'too materialistic and money loving' and so too 'busy earning money while leaving their children to their own devices'; third, by trying to silence their guilty consciences by offering their children more shopping money instead of their own time and care.

There is no doubt that the authors of the angry, condemnatory comments have a point. And yet there are also other, yet more powerful reasons why the numbers of girls like Georgie are rising. As Neal Lawson emphasizes in his remarkably perceptive and insightful study *All Consuming*,[7] the 'commercialisation of childhood has become a big driver of our turbo-consuming world' – but he also points out that children are only one of many territories invaded, conquered and colonized by the turbo-consumerism that is advancing simultaneously on many fronts. We *all*, or at any rate many and ever more of us, 'have been convinced that unless we keep up with the latest trends our lives are a failure'. And he adds: 'We buy things as signals of what we want to be and how we want others to think of us'. To sum up: 'what we bought became solidly entwined with our identity. Now we are what we buy.'

In other words, we can say that the mark of our time is a progressive effacement of the dividing line between acts of consumption and the rest of our life. We no longer go to shops in order to obtain an ingredient lacking for the soup we cook or to replace a pair of shoes worn beyond repair; there are now other, much less mundane, more sublime reasons for never staying away from the shops for long. All roads lead through the shops today – or so at least we are told, day in, day out, and on every occasion. Are you concerned with binding together and keeping intact your personal relations? 'Without others life is *nothing*' confirms the commercial of the newest edition of cellular phone, offering a new brand of portable not so much as a convenient means to transmit information, but as a contraption to make *something* out of your life. 'It's your watch that says the most about who you are' shouts another advert, addressed to all of us who feverishly seek the way to impress on people around us how should they see us and in what shape and form we wish to be 'consumed' by them. One commercial, for a novel car design, sums up all those suggestions and promises, stating bluntly: 'You buy [not a car but . . .] a piece of yourself.' What is intimated here, of course, is not a minor, small and insignificant 'piece' of yourself, but your public face, your image in the eyes of others, your interface with the world!

In this fast-moving world of ours, such precious 'pieces' need to be constantly updated; this is one of the prime reasons, by the way, for the mind-boggling popularity of 'social networking' internet sites like MySpace or Facebook, offering a perpetual, instant and almost effortless overhaul and updating of your face. As Felicia Wu Song found out in her recent doctoral study at the University of Virginia, 'many college students admit to being "addicted" to Facebook and leave the site permanently open on their computers. They check it right after they roll out of bed in the morning, while they study, and even in the middle of lectures on wireless campuses.' And, we may comment, they do it not just to satisfy idle curiosity, but to draw instant practical conclusions and set the agenda for the day (though not necessarily for tomorrow or next week). Wu Song concludes: 'Young Americans are comfortable approaching their personal relationships in the mode of *consumer*' (and, let me add, the mode of the *object of consumption* . . .).

Richard of Grand Rapids, USA, one of the attentive readers upset by what they learned from Diana Appleyard, wrote: 'Neither of my girls (9 and 13) wear any makeup, lipgloss, or obsess over food, clothing, cars, etc. They are healthy, proportional, and active. They have self-confidence without being narcissistic, and are overall really a joy to know. I attribute much of this to the fact that I actually spend time with the kids preparing meals, exercising together, helping them with homework, cleaning the house, etc. That – and the fact that we don't watch TV.'

Richard sounds proud of what he set out to achieve and what he has achieved thanks to keeping stubbornly to his resolution. And he has a right to feel proud: obviously, resisting pressures, withstanding tides, swimming against currents, ignoring overwhelming odds at your peril – all that requires courage and determination, as well as effective vaccination against the temptations of the comfort of being 'one of the crowd'. As Appleyard reminds us, 'it is almost impossible to stop ten-year-old girls from chatting to their friends, reading certain magazines and being obsessed about their figures.' And one more reason for Richard to feel proud: perhaps Richard has deprived his daughters of the (as Nietzsche suggested) intoxication and ecstasy derived from stampeding step by step, in step with a herd – but he has also spared them (as Bob Reitemeier, of the Children's Society, warned) 'being inundated with images they are not emotionally mature enough to cope with', and that may push them with every step closer to depression . . .

Well, all that is ultimately a matter of choice. Choice signals freedom. Freedom means taking risks. The risk Richard took is that his 9- and 13-year-old daughters might sooner or later turn the tables, and perceive and proclaim their freedom from stampeding herds and from the surfeit of images – the condition lovingly provided/enforced by their father – as another case of odious and repellent parental tyranny . . .

15

It is the eyelash's turn

Do you know what the name 'eyelash hypotrichosis' stands for? Until quite recently, most women lived happily not only in ignorance of the answer to that question, but without noticing their ignorance, let along worrying about it. Not much longer, though . . .

That the human body is in most cases far from perfect, and therefore needs to be tinkered and tampered with to help it to improve or force it to meet to the desired standards, is not news. Cosmetics is one of the oldest arts, and the supply of substances, tools, expedients and skills which the practising of that art requires or is believed to benefit from is one of the oldest industries. By an interesting coincidence, though, the beautification of the body was also one of those human preoccupations in which the appearance of a remedy as a rule preceded an awareness of the deficiency that was clamouring to be remedied. First came the good news: 'this *can* be done.' Thereafter, a commandment: 'you *must* do it!' And in the footsteps of the commandment, the threat of terrifying consequences (the penalty of stigma and shame!) for those who might dare to ignore it. The awareness that if you apply the remedy on offer you'll get rid of an abominable defect will descend on you as you begin to struggle to fulfil the commandment; it will arrive together with a fear that failing to struggle bravely enough and indefatigably enough will put you to shame – by unmasking and revealing to people around you your unforgivable incompetence, inaptitude, slatterliness and sloth.

The affair of eyelash hypotrichosis is just another instalment in that ancient but constantly replayed drama. Their eyelashes being too short, not dense enough, is not a condition women are likely to enjoy (as a matter of fact, most feel their eyelashes are too short and not dense enough; however long and dense their eyelashes may be, they could always be a bit longer and bushier – and it would be nice, wouldn't it, if they were). But few women would normally make a tragedy of that deficiency. Even fewer would consider it a disease, let alone an affliction calling for radical therapy, like breast cancer or infertility. One can bear with too few eyelashes: an ailment that can anyway be easily mitigated or covered up, whenever it matters, with a few brushes of mascara.

Not so, however, since the powerful pharmaceutical company Allergan (the same company that blessed wrinkle-fearing women with Botox filler) announced that faint and slender eyelashes had been diagnosed as the outcome of a condition *requiring medical intervention*; but that, fortunately, an *effective cure* for such a condition had been discovered and made available in the shape of a lotion called Latisse. Latisse is capable of making heretofore absent eyelashes sprout, and heretofore inconspicuous eyelashes grow longer and more telling; on one condition, though: that the lotion is used regularly, day in, day out – from now to eternity . . . If you interrupt the therapy – effective only if it is administered continuously – your eyelashes will revert to their previous abominable condition in no time. From the moment you learned that you could avoid it, but failed to do so, showing short and sparse eyelashes became a disgraceful and shameful act! Not just a question of vanity and cosmetics, but of loss of social esteem.

Catherine Bennett of the *Guardian* observed that many a doctor thinks and feels that 'women in their un-enhanced state offer plenty of scope for improvement' (and let me add: no less scope for continuously raising the income of medics and pharmacists). Indeed, cosmetic surgery has been one of the most rapidly growing industries in recent years (if *plastic* surgery, often confused with its 'cosmetic' cousin, is a speciality dedicated to the surgical repair of *defects* of form or function of bodily organs, *cosmetic* surgery is designed to improve the *appearance* of the body, not the body itself, and certainly not its health or fitness).

In 2006, 11 million cosmetic operations were performed in the US alone. It is enough to browse at random through a few websites to find out that a typical advertisement for cosmetic clinics, now a huge and highly lucrative industry, bristles with temptations which few if any women anxious about their appearance (and so, obliquely, about their social standing and socialite market value) would be able to resist:

> Whether you feel your breasts are too small and require a breast enlargement, or you want to rediscover the body which you had before having your family through liposuction or a tummy tuck, we can help find the right procedure for you. The effects of ageing can be reversed and features that have bothered you for years can be changed and a new physique can be attained, which could not be achieved even with exercise and a healthy diet.

Temptations are many, the net is cast wide, there is something for every worry and a worry for every woman, so that every or almost every woman will find at least one appeal which feels as if it has been addressed directly to her own personal self-respect and self-pride, pointing an accusing finger at her personally and personally censuring her for an unduly lukewarm approach to her duty.

For the face alone, clinics currently suggest a facelift, a cheek implant, nose surgery, ear correction, eyebag removal and chin implants; if the face seems to be OK, there is something that can be done to the breast – such as enlargement, reduction, uplift or nipple correction. Or for other parts of the body: liposuction, tummy tuck, buttock implants, calf implants, arm lift, thigh lift, vaginal tightening or 'gynecomastia'. A massive response to such commercials (and the moral pressure they arouse!) is well-nigh guaranteed. A few months before the recent 'credit crunch', in April 2008, William Saletan of NBC noted a trend towards

> making aesthetic procedures so safe and lucrative that people who would otherwise have devoted their careers to medicine turned instead to cosmetic work. Depending on how you count it, on an annual basis, the cosmetic-surgery industry – subset of the 'luxury healthcare sector' and parent of the 'facial aesthetics market' – is now worth $12 billion to $20 billion a year. Two weeks ago, the *New York Times* reported that last year, among 18 medical specialty fields, the three that attracted med-school seniors with the highest medical-board test scores were the most cosmetically oriented . . .

And so the story goes on repeating itself: an 'unenhanced' female body has been discovered to be a genuine, hitherto unfarmed (that is, bringing no profits because not wished to be 'enhanced') 'virgin land', a field laying fallow and for that reason more fertile than other, already exhausted plots of land, and promising much richer returns – land crying out for a clever, skilful and imaginative farming company to which it will guarantee, at least in the first years of exploitation, easy to obtain and profuse profits (even though, according to the economic law of diminishing returns, the profits will start to shrink as the investments swell). No square inch of a woman's body should be viewed as beyond improvement.

Life is insecure, a woman's life no less if not more than a man's, and that insecurity is potentially capital that won't placidly be left idle by any businessperson worthy of the name. As no amount of Latisse or Botox, however regularly applied, is likely to chase away that insecurity, the likes of Allergan can hope for steady and rising profits, and women can be sure of a long, indeed unending series of discoveries that what they believed to be a minor inconvenience is in fact a major menace that they must fight day and night and tooth and nail (with the help of the right kind of lotion or surgery, of course).

16

Fashion, or being on the move

Perpetuum mobile – a self-sustained and self-sufficient contraption containing everything needed to remain in continuous, uninterrupted movement, so eternally on the move, needing no further boost from the outside to stay in motion, no stimulus, push or pull, no intervention of an external force, no input of new energy . . .

At least since the time of Galileo and Newton, a perpetuum mobile was a dream of sages and mystics, tinkerers and tricksters alike. An object of feverish experimentation and a cause of endless frustration. Time and again its miraculous discovery or invention was announced, only to fail in demonstration, to be debunked as an illusion born of the dabbler's ignorance, or as a conman's hoax prompted by greed and abetted by spectators' gullibility; ending life as more footnotes in the long though as yet unfinished history of unreason. Ultimately, the idea of a perpetuum mobile landed on the rubbish heap of popular misconceptions, due not so much to the long string of disappointments as to the verdict of unfeasibility and sentence of capital punishment passed by modern physics.

There is no quarrelling with the physicists' pronouncements. When it comes to 'physical reality', and so also to the conditions of setting immobile bodies in motion, changing the velocity or direction of their movement, or bringing them to a standstill again, physicists have the last word which we have to accept in all humility. But at that other level of reality called 'social' – where bodies, while still being subject to laws of physics are indifferent to purpose and motives, fall in addition under the rule of purposeful change – things happen of which (as Shakespeare might have said) physicists wouldn't and couldn't dream. There in that other world, a perpetuum mobile – a self-triggered, self-propelled and self-sustained change, a movement prominent not so much by its inability to continue on its own as by its incapacity to grind to a halt, or even to slow down – suddenly becomes not only a possibility, but reality. Fashion is a crowning example of such an eventuality.

'About fashion', as Georg Simmel observed, 'one can't say that it "is". It is always becoming.'[8] In opposition to physical processes and yet in close affinity with the concept and ideal type of perpetuum mobile, what is inconceivable in the case of fashion is not the eventuality of endlessly keeping on the move (and continuing to work), but an interruption of the string of self-induced changes already begun. Indeed, the most astounding aspect of that extraordinary quality is the fact that the process of change does not lose its momentum while its work – its impact on the world in which it operates – is being done. Not only is the 'becoming' of fashion seemingly inexhaustible and unstoppable, but it acquires more and more impetus and ability to accelerate as the volume of its material, tangible impact, and the number of objects it affects, rises.

Were fashion just a run-of-the-mill physical process, it would be a monstrous anomaly, violating the laws of nature. But it is not a phenomenon of physics: it is a *social* phenomenon, and social life as a whole is a startling contraption with the power to suspend the operation of the second law of thermodynamics, carving out an enclave sheltered from the curse of entropy, that 'thermodynamic quantity' which represents (according to www. princeton.edu) 'the amount of energy in a system that is no longer available for doing mechanical work' and which 'increases as matter and energy in the universe degrade to an ultimate state of inert uniformity'. In the case of fashion, the 'inert uniformity' is not the 'ultimate state', and is indeed an ever more distant prospect. It is as if fashion were equipped with in-built safety valves that spring open well before the target of 'uniformity' – allegedly one of the essential human motives setting the process of fashion into its perpetual motion – comes too close for comfort, threatening to undermine or make null and void fashion's power of attraction and seduction. Entropy being, so to speak, a phenomenon of 'counter-differentiation', fashion – while drawing its impetus from the human tendency to resent difference and long for it to be levelled – manages to reproduce in constantly increasing volumes the self-same divisions, inequalities, discriminations and deprivations it has promised to mitigate, flatten, or even eliminate altogether.

An impossibility inside the physical universe, a *perpetuum mobile* is ushered into the realm of reality in the world of sociality, where it manages to become a norm. How can it be done? Simmel explains: by bringing together two equally powerful and overwhelming human urges or longings – companions that are never separable, yet are constantly at loggerheads with each other and pushing or pulling human undertakings in mutually opposite directions. Borrowing our metaphors once more from the vocabulary of physics, we may say that in the case of fashion the 'kinetic energy' of movement is gradually, yet completely transformed into a potential energy ready to turn into the kinetic energy of countermovement. The pendulum goes on swinging, and in principle can continue swinging indefinitely, by its own momentum.

The two human urges or longings in question are the longing to be part of a greater whole, and the urge of individualization or uniqueness; a dream of belonging and a dream of self-assertion; desire for social support and lust for autonomy; an impulse to imitation and a drive to separation. We may say, ultimately: a need for the *security* of holding hands, and for the *freedom* to let them go ... Or, to look at the same emotional coupling and dilemma from the opposite side: the fear of standing out and the horror of the self's dissolution.

Just like many (most?) married couples, security and freedom cannot live without each other, yet find living together a daunting task. Security without freedom is a sentence to slavery, while freedom without security is a condemnation to nerve-breaking and incurable uncertainty. When deprived of the compensation or limitation of their partner (or, rather, of their 'alter ego'), both security and freedom turn from coveted values into terrifying nightmares. Security and freedom need, and can't endure, one another, simultaneously desire and resent each other, though the proportions of the two contradictory sentiments change with each of the frequent (frequent enough to be deemed routine) departures from the 'golden mean' of a (temporarily) equilibrating settlement.

Attempts at balancing and reconciling them prove to be incomplete as a rule, stopping short of full satisfaction, and most importantly too shaky and frail to exude an air of finality. There are always some loose ends needing to be tied up, yet every time they are pulled they threaten to tear up the delicately woven social network. For that reason, attempts at reconciliation will never reach their explicitly or implicitly pursued purpose, manifest or latent; though all the same they will never be – they can't be – abandoned. This is why the cohabitation of security and freedom is bound to stay full of sound and fury. Its endemic and irresolvable ambivalence makes of it an inexhaustible source of creative energy and obsessive change. For the same reason, it is predestined to be a *perpetuum mobile*.

'Fashion', says Simmel, 'is a peculiar form of life which is to secure a compromise between the tendency to social levelling and the tendency to individual uniqueness.' That compromise, let's recall, can't be a 'stable state'. It can't be established once and for all: the clause 'until further [as a rule abominably short!] notice' is engraved indelibly on its mode of existence. That compromise, just like the fashion itself, is always 'becoming'. It can't stay put and needs to be perpetually renegotiated. Triggered by the impulse of one-upmanship (see the Introduction to my *Art of Life*),[9] the pursuit of the (currently) fashionable quickly leads to making tokens of distinction banal and common – so that the briefest moment of inattention or the slightest slowing (not to mention negligence) of the pace of change may swiftly bring about an effect opposite to the ones intended: the loss of individuality. New tokens need to be rapidly obtained, yesterday's tokens need to be immediately and ostentatiously rushed to the dump. The precept of 'what is no longer on' needs to be as meticulously observed and as diligently obeyed as the precept of 'what is new and (currently) on the way up'. A life status indicated, communicated and recognized by the acquisition and display of (short-lived and infuriatingly changeable) tokens of fashion is defined in equal measure by tokens on conspicuous display and tokens conspicuous by their absence. In Hadley Freeman's succinct yet poignant summary in the *Guardian* of 9 September 2009, 'the fashion industry is not interested in making women feel better about themselves. Fashion is about making people want something they are unlikely to get . . . and any satisfaction achieved is fleeting and faintly disappointing.'

The perpetuum mobile of fashion is thus the dedicated, dexterous and seasoned destroyer of every and any standstill. Fashion casts lifestyles in the mode of permanent, unfinishable revolution. Given that the phenomenon of fashion is intimately and inseparably linked to two 'eternal' and 'universal' attributes of the human way of being-in-the-world and their equally irreparable incompatibility, its ubiquitous presence is not confined to one, or some selected, forms of life. At any time in human history and on any territory of human habitation, it plays a crucial operating role in rendering constant change into the norm of the human way of being-in-the-world. The way in which it operates, however, and the institutions that sustain and service it do change from one form of life to another.

The present-day variety of the fashion phenomenon is determined by the colonization and exploitation of that eternal aspect of human condition by the *consumer markets*.

17

Consumerism is not just about consumption

We are all consumers, obviously – as long as we live. It can't be otherwise: if we stop consuming, we'll die, the only moot question being how many days it will take. Consumption (meaning, according to the *Oxford English Dictionary*, 'to use up', 'to eat up', to drink up', and so to 'take up', 'spend', 'waste away', 'burn away') is a necessity. But 'consumerism' – that tendency to assign concerns with consumption as the place of the royal way to pursue all other concerns, and all too often the distinction of the ultimate target of such pursuits – is not.

Consumerism is a *social* product, not the non-negotiable verdict of *biological* evolution. It is not enough to consume merely to stay alive if your wish is to live and act according to consumerism's rules. Consumerism is more, much more than mere consumption. Consumerism serves many purposes. Consumerism is a multipurpose and multifunctional phenomenon: a sort of a skeleton key opening every and any lock, a fully and truly universal gadget. Consumerism means transforming human beings into consumers first and foremost, and demoting all their other aspects to secondary, derivative and inferior ranks. Consumerism also means the recycling of biological necessity into commercial capital. Sometimes into political capital as well.

Let me explain what I mean by that. To start with, an early message sent by President George W. Bush to Americans shocked and stupefied by the sight of twin emblems of American world rule crumbling, having been perforated by aircraft guided by terrorists, was 'to go back shopping'. The message was intended to be understood as a call to return to *normal* life. Well before the enemy struck, Americans must already have been made to assume that shopping was the way (perhaps the sole, and certainly the paramount way) to cure every affliction, repel and push back any menace, and repair all malfunctions. Choosing shopping as a proper response to a novel, unheard-of and totally unfamiliar challenge, and thus one that was exceptionally horrifying, stupefying and disorienting, was therefore the simplest and surest way to reduce a horrid event to the lowly rank of an ordinary annoyance: disenchanting, taming, familiarizing and domesticating it, and (last but not least) draining it of its venom. 'Go shopping' meant: we are back to normal. Business as usual. As in so many other cases, less dramatic though no less consequential (such as, for instance, the periodical fall in GNP – that is, of the amount of money changing hands, the official measure of the level of economic prosperity of the country; or the creeping horror of an approaching, impending economic recession), salvation was expected to result from consumers' decisions to resume the diligent fulfilment of their duty to shop and spend money they had earned or hoped to earn – after a hopefully brief interval of belt-tightening. That it is up to consumers to 'save the country from falling into depression' or to 'lead the country out of the recession' has turned into a dogma we hardly ever question: one of the pillars of popular wisdom and common sense. As the meaning of 'citizenship' moves steadily towards a model of a dutiful consumer, so the meaning of 'patriotism' follows by shifting towards a model of earnest and dedicated shopping.

This is not, however, the only use to which the humdrum, humble need to consume has been put in a consumerist society like ours. It is only a sample drawn from a vast category of problems that we confront, are warned that we will soon confront or told we have already confronted; problems where the most widely used road to their solution has been diverted to lead, unswervingly and obligatorily, through the shops. The archetype for this extensive and unstoppably swelling category of shopping-related resolutions of problems is provided by physical illness, for which we seek a remedy in the pharmacy. In a consumerist society, we can say that all shops and service outlets are first and foremost *pharmacies* – whatever, rather than drugs, they display on their shelves and stands and put on sale for present and prospective customers.

Whatever the other, ostensible uses of the goods on sale, most of the goods are (or at least they are suggested and imagined to be) *medicines*. Obtaining such goods and consuming them are acts conjectured and hoped to placate discomforts or pains which would otherwise go on seething and festering; or better still, acts expected to prevent the displeasures which are certain to descend upon the slothful or negligent shopper. All sorts of discomforts: not just the need to refill the wardrobe or refrigerator that serves your routine daily consumption, or the cyclical replenishment of used-up or worn-out stocks, but also the fear of losing your 'market value' and falling out of 'social circulation': losing esteem, popularity, company, even friends – all because you have lagged behind the current talk of the town and its most avidly played games, and so have been ignorant of, and failed to obtain the things the people around you are now most eagerly talking about and most keen on doing. In short, the grave discomfort(s) caused by overlooking the fact that other people have come across new inventions or discoveries capable of offering sensations and satisfactions of which you – having missed the moment of their arrival – might be sorely deprived. Or a constantly simmering uncertainty about the topicality of the knowledge and skills you've acquired in the past but still, imprudently, deploy in the present: a gnawing suspicion that such knowledge and skills, like everything else in this fast-moving world, may need to be urgently updated and overhauled.

Confidence that you have kept up with the hectic pace of change, and so are still in the right, needs new proofs and new reassurance every day. A regular stroll through a shopping mall may be the answer to all these anxieties: it may reassure you that you are still on the right track, and can help you to stay in the game. The most poignant of the discomforts, a sort of metadiscomfort that underpins all the other, more specific discomforts, and prompts you to endlessly repeat your visits to consumerist pharmacies, is the uncertainty about being in the right – about whether your preferences are set as they should be according to current evaluations, about making the right choices, doing the right things and behaving in the right way.

Orthodox pharmacies, the old-style and by now old-fashioned chemist shops, promised to mitigate pain and alleviate other bodily discomforts. You went to the chemist to obtain a medicine for a sore throat, a runny nose, back pain or heartburn: there was nothing uncertain about the pain that prompted you to run to the pharmacist for advice and help. But if the present-day consumerist pharmacies were foolishly to count only on victims of no uncertain suffering, the ranks of their regular customers would be decimated. Happily, they don't commit this folly. They take care that Shakespeare's 'inaudible and noiseless foot of time' be neither noiseless nor, God forbid, inaudible. The foot of time now shouts from every TV screen and headphone, every page of every glossy magazine – and from every conversation of their voluntary or involuntary, unpaid (ironically, paying!) yet brave and militant mercenaries, and similarly unpaid yet dedicated and hard-working agents. In defiance of Shakespeare, the 'foot of time' is no longer to be unheard. The sounds emitted by its plodding or strutting are an alarm signal: never forget that time has feet, nimble, sprightly and fast, and (as Lewis Carroll prophetically warned) you need to run as quickly as you can just to stay where you are . . .

In a consumerist society, the sounds of the scurrying and scampering feet of time hammer home one message: it is not just the things you are uncertain about that require your immediate attention, but things you do not yet know you are uncertain about. This sounds an ultimate, irrevocable and unmistakable death knell to all and any certainty. All certainty being putative and at best until further notice, all self-confidence being a product of insufficient attention or downright ignorance, the most treacherous variety of uncertainty is the uncertainty that haunts you the least or not at all, uncertainty of which you, perilously, are as yet unaware . . .

Fortunately for us all, willing or unwilling prisoners of consumerism, consumerist pharmacies are tightly packed together along high streets and their innumerable, ever more sophisticated and ubiquitous extensions, to provide the life-belts and life-saving services you need: to free you of the uncertainty you know and to open your eyes to the uncertainties you don't.

18
Whatever happened to the cultural elite?

Pierre Bourdieu, the great French sociologist, suggested 30 years ago (in his highly influential book *Distinction*) that the 'cultural elite', people believed to carry the highest authority when it comes to drawing the difference between *comme il faut* and *comme il ne faut pas* (how it should be, and how it shouldn't) in all things 'cultural', were set apart from the rest of us by their highly selective artistic taste and strictly defined standards – in stark opposition to our common undiscerning taste and absence or blatant laxity of standards. It was that contrast that sustained the division between 'high culture' (approved and practised by the cultural elite) and the 'low (popular or mass) culture' of the rest.

According to a report written by Andy McSmith and published in the online edition of the *Independent*, authoritative academics in a very authoritative (Oxford) university have proclaimed that the 'cultural elite does not exist' in the old sense.[10] Tak Wing Chan and John Goldthorpe, Oxford researchers in social science, and a team of 13 have concluded from data collected from the UK, Chile, France, Hungary, Israel, the Netherlands and the US that what can no longer be found is a 'cultural elite' of the kind described by Bourdieu – top people distinguishing themselves from their inferiors by going to the opera and admiring whatever has currently been branded 'high art', while turning up their noses at, and treating with overt contempt 'anything as vulgar as a pop song or mainstream television'.

As a matter of fact, the demise of the *old-style* elite (but not of the 'cultural elite' as such!) is not news. As long ago as 1992, to grasp the nature of taste (or rather the absence of taste) typical of the 'cultural leaders' of the time, Richard A. Petersen of Vanderbilt University used the metaphor of 'omnivorousness'[11]: opera *and* pop songs, 'high art' *and* mainstream television; a bit from here, a morsel from there, now this, now that. And Petersen recently restated his original discovery: 'we see a shift in elite status group politics from those highbrows who snobbishly disdain all base, vulgar, or mass popular culture... to those highbrows who omnivorously consume a wide range of popular as well as high-brow art forms.'[12] In other words: *Nihil* 'cultural' *a me alienum puto*, there is nothing 'cultural' I'd reject offhand without tasting it, though there is nothing 'cultural' either with which I'd identify unswervingly and uncompromisingly to the exclusion of other enjoyments. I am *everywhere at home*, though (or because) that somewhere I'd call *my home is nowhere*. All in all, it is no longer one (refined) taste against another (vulgar) one. It is omnivorous-ness against univorousness, a readiness to consume-it-all and savour-it-all against discretion, any *a priori* selectiveness of appre-ciation, disgust or incomprehension. The elite is alive and well, livelier and busier than ever before, though too engrossed in chasing and consuming all things cultural to have any time left for a missionary preoccupation with proselytizing and converting. Apart from 'stop fussing, be less selective' and 'consume more', that elite in its latest reincarnation has no message to convey to the crowds of univores lower down in the cultural hierarchy. To all practical intents and purposes, it has washed its hands of any vocation to convert, proselytize, enlighten, ennoble and altogether 'uplift' the 'people' (rebranded as the 'masses', or, more to the point, 'cultural consumers').

Indeed, in those parts where pleas on behalf of culture are composed, voiced and debated, the arts have lost (or at any rate are fast losing) their function as a handmaiden of a social hierar-chy struggling to self-reproduce – just as some time earlier culture as a whole lost its original function as a handmaiden of emergent nations, states and class hierarchies. The arts are now free to serve *individual* concerns with self-identification and self-assertion.

We can say that, in its liquid modern phase, culture (and most conspicuously its artistic branch) is made to the measure of *individual* freedom of choice (willingly pursued, or endured as obligatory). And that it is *intended* to service such freedom. And that it is intended to see to it that the choice remains *unavoidable*: a life necessity, and a duty. And that responsibility, the inalienable companion of free choice, stays where the liquid modern condition has forced it: on the shoulders of the *individual*, now appointed the sole manager of individually conducted 'life politics'.

As befits a society of consumers like ours, culture today consists of *offers*, not *norms*. Just as Bourdieu noted, culture lives by seduction, not normative regulation: public relations, not policing; creating new needs, desires, wants and whims, not coercion. This society of ours is a society of consumers, and just like the rest of the world as consumers see and live it, culture becomes a warehouse of products meant for consumption – each vying for the floating, shifting and drifting attention of prospective consumers in the hope of attracting it, and catching and holding it for a bit longer than a fleeting moment. Abandoning rigid standards, indulging lack of discrimination, serving all tastes while privileging none, encouraging fitfulness and 'flexibility' (the popular and politically correct name for spinelessness) and romanticizing unsteadiness and inconsistency, all these therefore combine into the proper (the only reasonable? the only feasible?) strategy to follow. Fastidiousness, a raising of the eyebrows, a stiffening of upper lips are not recommended. An influential TV reviewer and critic praised a New Year's Eve broadcast in 2007–8 for promising 'to provide an array of musical entertainment guaranteed to sate everyone's appetite'. 'The good thing' about it, he explained, 'is that its universal appeal means you can dip in and out of the show depending on your preferences'.[13] A commendable and indeed seemly quality in a society in which networks replace structures while the attachment/detachment game and an unending procession of connections and disconnections replace 'determining' and 'fixing'.

Culture is now turning into one of the departments in the 'all you need and dream of' department store into which the world inhabited by consumers has turned. As in other departments of that store, the shelves are tightly packed with constantly restocked commodities, while the counters are adorned with commercials for the latest offers – themselves destined soon to disappear together with the attractions they advertise. The commodities and

commercials alike are calculated to arouse desires and trigger
wishes for the new offers while stifling any desire or wish to hold
on to the old (as George Steiner famously put it, they are calculated for 'maximum impact and instant obsolescence'). Merchants
and copywriters count on wedding the seductive power of offers
to the ingrained 'one-upmanship' and urge of their prospective
customers to 'get an edge', or at least keep pace with the
'style-pack'.

Liquid modern culture has no 'people' to 'cultivate'. It has
instead *clients* to *seduce*. And unlike its 'solid modern' predecessor, it no longer wishes to work itself out of a job, eventually, but
the sooner the better. Its job is now to render its own survival
permanent – through making temporary all aspects of life of its
former wards and prospective converts, now reborn as clients.

19

Drugs and diseases

The idea of 'disease' is known to all cultures and languages; for time immemorial, there has been and survives a semantically equivalent word in every language, referring, as the word '*dis*-ease' does, to an absence of 'ease': to a psychical or bodily *dis*-comfort, *in*-convenience, *in*-firmity, *dis*-tress. That word says that the condition of the person to whom it applies is not what it ought to be, or what it is *normally* expected to be. Disease means *ab*-normality of the *dis*-eased person's condition.

In its contemporary usage, the term 'disease' (illness, sickness) tends however to be used interchangeably with the concept of 'medical condition'. This other concept only pretends to be an equivalent of the first, however: it imports an added meaning on the sly – and a crucial one, switching the whole issue of 'lack of ease' to another register altogether: from a *condition* to an *action* which that condition is presumed or alleged to call for. In fact, it gives the action undertaken, or about to be undertaken, the power to define the condition it is meant to tackle: nowadays it is once medics enter the stage that the drama being played out is that of a disease.

The concept of a 'medical condition' thereby pre-empts the issue which otherwise could have been a subject for debate and perhaps contention – the issue as to whether the *condition* in question is ripe for, and amenable to, *medical* intervention. It assumes that it has been already decided ('it is obvious') that a doctor is bound to be visited or called on to visit, that medical tests are to be carried out, medicine is to be prescribed, obtained and consumed, and a treatment regime is to be followed. It reconfirms, even if in a roundabout way, that the medical and pharmaceutical professions are and should be in charge and in control of the ill person's body and mind. When we perceive disease to be identical with 'medical condition' (and so, obliquely yet forcefully, to be a projection of the act of medical intervention), the fact of being ill is defined by the circumstance of being subject to, eligible for and demanding a medical action. 'Being sick' now means asking for a doctor's help; while a doctor offering help determines that the condition is that of a disease . . . What comes first, the egg or the chicken? And which of the two facts is the chicken, and which one is the egg?

As Marcia Angell has suggested, reviewing three new book-length studies in the *New York Review of Books* (15 January 2009), 'in recent years, drug companies have perfected a new and highly effective method to expand their markets. Instead of promoting drugs to treat diseases, they have begun to promote diseases to fit their drugs.' The new strategy is 'to convince Americans that there are only two kinds of people: those with medical conditions that require drug treatment and those who don't know it yet'.

Let me point out, though, that it was not necessarily the drug companies that invented and developed this new strategy. More likely, the drug companies have followed the universal trend in present-day marketing practice. These days, the offer of new commodities no longer follows existing demand: *demand must be created for commodities already launched on the market, thereby following the logic of a commercial company in search of profit, rather than the logic of human needs in search of satisfaction.* This new trend could get into full swing only once the idea had been insinuated and entrenched in our minds that there is and can be no limit to the level of our self-perfecting exploits, and to the satisfactions brought by further rises in that level. However wonderful your present condition, it can and it should be made better still . . .

If the vision of the state of *health* has not only a bottom but also a top limit, allowing you to relax once you've reached it, the quality of *fitness* that came to replace it or push it into a

secondary position among our contemporary concerns, has no
limits: the struggle for fitness, unlike the care for health in its
received, orthodox sense, will never finish and you will never be
permitted to slacken your exertions. However fit you are, you can
always be fitter; your sensual satisfactions could always be more
satisfactory than they are at the moment, pleasures more pleasur-
able and delights more delightful. The ingenuity of drug companies boils down to a *harnessing of the authority and persuasive
powers of a concern for health to a pursuit of ever rising fitness
and self-approval* – which we, consumers in a society of consumers, are nudged, persuaded and trained to follow. It has already
become part of our life philosophy – or indeed our common sense
– that the road to greater fitness and more self-approval must lead
through careful study of the newest commercials, and that it is
bound to end in the shops. And in becoming an integral part of
common sense, that is turning into one of those things that 'everybody knows', 'everybody accepts' and 'everybody does', it has
been converted into the main and inexhaustible resource in companies' scramble for profits and ever more profits.

It does not matter much whether the condition against which
the newly introduced drug promises to act is serious – pregnant
with grave consequences, genuinely threatening and profoundly
discomforting its victims. What matters much more is how
common that condition is – and therefore how numerous are the
drug's prospective consumers and therefore how large the company's prospective profits. According to that principle, afflictions
most of us are accustomed to bearing with routinely and almost
daily (such as heartburn, premenstrual tension or – indeed – that
all-too-common deficit of self-confidence rebounding as shyness)
have recently been redefined as diseases: given learned, all too
often bizarre and incomprehensible, and for that reason ominous-
sounding names (heartburn, for instance, is likely to be referred
to by your doctor or pharmacist as 'gastro-aesophageal reflux
disease'), and therefore requiring urgent medical attention.

Christopher Lane has traced the spectacular recent medical and
pharmaceutical career of one of most widespread aspects of human
life: the experience of protracted or momentary shyness (which of
us can say, hand on heart, that she or he never felt timid,
chary or diffident?!). That common and frequently experienced
unpleasantness is now known in medical practice under the more

serious-sounding name of 'social anxiety disorder'. In 1980 it was described in the authoritative *Diagnostic and Statistical Manual of Mental Disorders* – still under the name of 'social phobia', now abandoned – as 'rare'. In 1994, it was reclassified as 'extremely common'. By 1999, the pharmaceutical giant GlaxoSmithKline had launched a multimillion dollar anxiety-promoting campaign to create a market for its drug Paxil, which was guaranteed to alleviate or even put paid to that (as the commercials now put it) 'severe medical condition'. Lane quotes Barry Brand, Paxil's product director: 'Every marketer's dream is to find an unidentified or unknown market and develop it. That's what we were able to do with social anxiety disorder.'

Of course, what we pay for in such cases is the promised freedom from a *particular* fear and anxiety, but seldom if ever does the drug we buy make us *generally* less fearful and less prone to anxiety. Once we accept that for every affliction and discomfort caused by the ordinary trials and tribulations of life there is (there must be, there surely will be) a drug to be obtained in the nearest pharmacy, that frustrated potential of the allegedly 'life-enhancing' drugs remains a source of endless disappointment for their consumers and also of endless gains for their advertisers, distributors and sellers. Ironically, we are even manoeuvred into financing our disappointments. Each drug newly introduced to replace its already discredited predecessor tends to be sold at a higher price (following the pattern of toys in Aldous Huxley's dystopia of the *Brave New World*) – an increase hardly justified by its added effectiveness . . .

Swine flu and other reasons to panic

I can't be sure whether, when you read these words, you'll be still frightened by the spectre of the 'swine flu' virus crossing the Atlantic from Mexico to reach your door; and whether you will be as frightened by that prospect as the people around me are (or are pressed to be) now, when I am writing them. I am not even sure whether you'll still remember what all that panic was about. After all, a major task of the headlines in daily papers is to efface from memory last week's headlines – and so to clear the site of public attention, making room for next week's ones. And as for the panics, the more awesome and intense they are, the more rapidly they exhaust our supplies of passion and their own powers of curdling the blood and fraying the nerves, so that wholly new kinds of juicy and scary, newspaper-selling and ratings-enhancing headlines are urgently needed to beef up lagging newspaper circulations and thinning TV audiences. For all such reasons and more, I can't be sure what it is that you are currently panicking about when you read these words. And I suspect you may feel that what I am writing now is an ancient story, a case long shut (if it was ever open), nothing worth wasting time on and concerning oneself with. Perhaps you now have other reasons to be frightened and so have neither the time nor the room in your mind for old fears.

To be sure, even as I write these words, the front pages of newspapers are already spattered with other alerting, alarming and panic-inspiring headlines. The news of the progress of swine flu has moved to minor pages, reappearing only sporadically, and the type in which it is printed has lost much of its recent height and thickness. And when the news is printed, it tends to be accompanied (unlike a few days ago) by a mixture of amazement, scepticism and irony. For instance, Bart Laws, a medical officer at Tufts Medical Centre in Boston, observes melancholically that the authorities who issued a pandemic alert 'have just done what they are supposed to do. It is possible, but not at all likely, that this virus will cause an unusual amount of trouble' – but adds right away, however, that 'it is much more likely that it [the panic] will fade away in a couple of weeks, because the flue season is nearly over, and there is no evidence that there is anything unusual about the way this virus behaves.' A summary of recent events by Simon Jenkins of the *Guardian* is yet more sceptical and sarcastic and reaches deeper to the real core of the trouble: 'The [virus] mutation did have worrying features. But nothing justified the pandemonium of UK authorities and media.'

We know already that the number of people killed in Mexico by the brand-new mutation of the flu virus was no higher than the average annual toll of flu victims, and many times smaller than the number of people killed annually in road accidents (around 12,000 people die of flu each year worldwide; in the US, about 150 children are killed by influenza every year, and that compares with 7,677 children killed in motorway crashes in 2003 alone, and 3,001 murdered). As for the people who visited Mexico at the time the new mutation was identified, and were watched with suspicion and horror after their return home as carriers of planetary pandemics – many more (routinely, for visitors to Mexico) fell victim to food poisoning. But we know as well that 32 million masks were ordered (and stored, found useless, and are bound soon to be removed from warehouses to make room for other supplies for a 'rainy day') by the British government, all too aware that the precept 'better safe than sorry' is a must which no government wishing to survive the next election can ignore; and that to be shown by thousands of TV cameras on millions of TV screens to be passionately 'busy in action', spying out clandestine plots, creeping threats and invisible menaces, and valiantly fighting back against them, is a condition *sine qua non* these days of any government's survival.

More millions of pounds were spent on stocking hospitals and doctors' surgeries with Oseltamivir, a drug produced and marketed by the pharmaceutical giant Hoffmann–La Roche under the name of Tamiflu. As recently as 6 September 2009, Robin McKie, the science editor of the *Guardian*, informed us that the project 'to stockpile billions of doses of essential medicines in readiness for the swine flu epidemic' is worth tens of millions of pounds to drug companies, which have been asked to ensure there are stocks of penicillin, morphine, diazepam and insulin in case a major flu outbreak shuts down the country's pharmaceutical manufacturing and distribution network. This decision to stockpile medicines has been made despite the recent announcement by the government's most senior doctor that the expected second wave of swine flu will not be as bad as was feared.

It is public money that has been spent, money collected by taxes under threat of punitive sanctions from those who were scared and those who resisted scaremongering alike. A collusion between politicians and businessmen? Perhaps – though not necessarily by the politicians' free choice. Governments, after all, must demonstrate to their electors that they are daily protecting their lives and welfare from unspeakable disasters – from an interminably long line of variegated mortal threats and forms of perdition. This is why Sir Liam Donaldson, Chief Medical Officer in Britain, warned the nation that all optimism is premature and that swine flu 'could be expected to return' next winter, while a 'public health emergency' has been declared by authorities in many states of the US. This is also why the American vice-president Joe Biden has appealed to the nation not to ride on the subway or to board planes, painting a likeness of imminent disaster in the darkest and most frightening of colours. One way or another, scaremongering is now, as Jenkins comments, 'meat and drink to the booming empires of counterterrorism and "health and safety" . . . Crying wolf over globalised disease is now so much a part of the medical/ industrial complex that no sane person can tell what is real from what is log-rolling'. Indeed, we are all frightened into being frightened. Against the chorus of the stentorian prophets of doom, who would be bold and cheeky, foolish and heedless enough to blow the whistle, call their bluff and aver that the risk has been, by and large, invented, grossly exaggerated or blown up to absurd proportions – and can be safely ignored?

As far as silencing the opposition and the voices of reason goes, the virus has the great advantage of being invisible, and so the strongest viewing glasses cannot make us sure that the air we breathe is virus-free. We, the addressees of the alerts, the people called on and prodded (as well as being amenable) to panic, have no right of entry to the research and development laboratories from which the news of the vicious mutation arrives. We have a choice: trust the experts, the people 'in the know', or . . . Precisely: or WHAT?

Simon Jenkins finished his summary by expressing his certainty that 'when the current scare is over and the bill tallied, surely there will be an inquiry into this fiasco'. He does not believe, though, that an inquiry would prevent other similarly costly panics from happenning, as he suggests that we should listen to Voltaire's old advice and shoot a virologist from time to time to discourage others . . . The utter inhumanity of such advice apart, I doubt the wisdom of following it. After all, humble virologists do their jobs. It is the job of other people – high and mighty people – to make us frightened of their findings. Or of what they say their findings are. And to make some political or commercial gain in the process. And to score some precious personal Brownie points and profits on the way . . .

21
Health and inequality

Palm Beach is a narrow island in Florida, roughly 13 miles long, with a little more than 10,000 residents. Three bridges connect it to the mainland, but the residents feel and act as if the place was one big 'gated community'.

This is, to be sure, a kind of gated community that can manage without walls and barbed wire. House prices will do the job perfectly well, thank you. The few houses currently on the market are priced from 700,000 to 72.5 million dollars. Palm Beach is, by common agreement, the site of the highest density of wealth in the whole of the United States – more millions per square mile than anywhere else. The local joke is that calling a resident a 'millionaire' here is an insult. In the boutiques along Worth Avenue, the street where Palm Beach residents acquire their attire, a sweater will cost you a thousand dollars, and a pair of trousers may set you back by twice as much. To belong to the local country club, you'll pay 300,000 dollars just as the joining fee. As David Segal of the *New York Times* estimated, the losses suffered by Palm Beach residents in the course of the recent stock exchange crash, in line with Palm Beach's unique status, have also been unparalleled elsewhere in the US. 'The net worth of the average resident', he suggests, 'has recently plunged . . . by more than the average net worth in any other town or city in the country.' This, probably more than any other statistic, certifies the exclusive position, all its own, occupied by Palm Beach at the top of the American (and perhaps planetary) wealth league.

In Palm Beach there is not a single cemetery, funeral parlour or hospital. Death and illness have been all but chased out of the minds of Palm Beach residents (though not, of course, out of their lives, despite all their earnest, dedicated trying, with no money spared), even though many of them are well into their eighties.

In Britain, a team of researchers led by Domenico Pagano of the Birmingham Hospital Trust traced the fate of about 45,000 patients with an average age of 65 who underwent heart surgery. They found that the number of deaths following the surgery depended heavily on the patients' wealth and shot up as income fell: among the poor, many more patients die. The 'usual suspects', smoking, obesity and diabetes – all known to affect the poor more than the well-off – were promptly called to account; but to no avail. When allowances were made for their probable impact on mortality statistics, the sharp difference in post-op survival rates remained. The only conclusion possible was that if the poor among the patients of heart surgery had less chance of survival than the better-off, it was just courtesy of their poverty . . .

Until not so long ago, the idea that rising prosperity at the top would eventually benefit the whole of the rest of society through a kind of 'trickle-down' effect was part of the commonsense wisdom keenly cultivated by political leaders of all or almost all political hues. But such a 'trickle-down' effect is not currently to be found anywhere, if it ever was; the link between the elite getting richer and the life of the community as a whole getting safer and healthier is a figment of the imagination – and, not to hide a pig in a poke, of political propaganda. Yet more to our point, as Richard Wilkinson and Kate Pickett have amply documented and proved beyond reasonable doubt in their book *The Spirit Level*,[14] the summary or the average *wealth of a nation* as measured by gross national product has little impact on a long list of social evils, while the way in which that wealth is distributed, in other words the degree of *social inequality*, profoundly influences the spread and intensity of those evils. For instance, Japan and Sweden are countries run in very different ways, Sweden with a big welfare state and Japan with very little state-administered social provision; what unites them, however, is a relatively even spread of incomes and so also a relatively small gap between the living standards of the top fifth and the bottom fifth of the population; and, remarkably, fewer 'social problems' than in other affluent industrialized countries with a less equitable division of income and wealth. Another example is offered by two close and intimately connected neighbours, Spain and Portugal, the second with indices of social inequality almost double those of the first: in the number and the intensity of its 'social problems', Portugal beats Spain hands down!

In the most unequal societies on the planet, such as the US or Britain, the incidence of mental illness is three time higher than at the bottom of the inequality league; their prison populations are also much larger, as are the bane of obesity, the number of teenage pregnancies and (for all their summary wealth!) the death rates for *all* social classes, including the richest. Whereas the general level of health is as a rule higher in wealthier countries, among countries with more equality in wealth, death rates fall in proportion to the degree to which social equality rises. A truly striking and thought-provoking finding is that rising levels of expenditure specifically for *health* have almost no impact on average life expectancy, but a rising *level of inequality* does have such an impact, and a strongly negative one.

Why is this the case, ask the authors of this research. And they suggest that in an unequal society the fear of losing social position, of being degraded, socially excluded, denied dignity and humiliated is much stronger – and above all much more harrowing and horrifying, in view of the depth of the fall it signals. Such fears generate a lot of anxiety and make people more vulnerable to psychological disturbance and prone to mental depression, a factor that in turn takes its toll on life expectancy; particularly so among the middle classes, notoriously unsure of the durability of their achievements and the solidity of their privilege.

The list of acknowledged 'social ills' tormenting the so-called 'developed societies' is long, and despite all genuine or putative efforts it is growing longer. In addition to the few afflictions already mentioned, it contains items like homicide, infant mortality, and absence of mutual trust, without which social cohesion and cooperation are inconceivable. In each case the scores get more favourable as we move from more to less unequal societies; sometimes the differences are truly staggering. The United States is at the top of the inequality league, Japan at the very bottom. In the US, almost 500 people per 100,000 are in jail, in Japan fewer than 50 per 100,000. In the US, one-third of the population suffers from obesity, in Japan less than 10 per cent. In the US, of a thousand women aged 15–17, more than 50 are pregnant; in Japan, just three. In the US, more than a quarter of the population suffer from mental illness; in Japan, Spain, Italy and Germany, societies with a relatively more equal distribution of wealth, one in ten people reports a mental health problem, as against one in five in more unequal countries like Britain, Australia, New Zealand or Canada.

These are all statistics: summary counts or averages, along with their correlations. They say little about the causal connections behind those correlations. But they prod the imagination and sound an alert (at least they can alarm us, and should do). They appeal to the conscience *as well as* to instincts for survival. They challenge (and hopefully sap) our all-too-common ethical slumber and moral indifference; but they also show, beyond reasonable doubt, that the idea that the pursuit of the good life and happiness is a self-referential business is grossly misconceived and misleading. That the hope that one can 'do it alone', repeating Baron Münchausen's feat of extracting oneself from the bog by pulling at one's own wig, is a fatal mistake which defies the purpose of self-concern and self-care.

We can't get nearer to that purpose while distancing ourselves from other people's misfortunes. Our fight against 'social ills' can only be conducted together – or lost.

22

Be warned

When (if) it comes to the crunch and the next disaster strikes, neither you nor I would have the right to apologize that we hadn't been warned. Only someone like Simon the Hermit, spending his life perched on the top of a pole far above the madding crowds and beyond the reach of their chatter (if a similar feat were at all conceivable on a planet criss-crossed with information highways; contemporary followers of Simon the Hermit, were there any, would hardly remove the iPhone from their pockets before climbing the pole), could claim ignorance; not us, though, carrying smart contraptions in our palms offering on demand any knowledge there is to be known.

We know only too well, for instance, that we are sitting on an ecological time-bomb (even though signs of that knowledge being reflected in the ways we behave every day are few and far between). We are told over and over again that we are sitting on a demographic time-bomb ('too many of us, but particularly of "them", whoever "they" are . . .'). Or a consumerist time-bomb ('for how long can our poor planet sustain those millions knocking at our doors begging and hoping to be allowed to join our feast?'). And quite a few other bombs as well, their numbers rising rather than showing the slightest sign of a reduction. So you won't be particularly shocked by a warning that among all those bombs there is one ticking no less ominously that those mentioned, yet somehow earning still less of our attention than the other ones do.

A few weeks ago we could have heard one such warning (but how many of us listened?): about the *inequality time-bomb*, likely to explode in the not too distant future. A United Nations report on current urban developments, based on a study of 120 major cities of the world, warned that 'high levels of inequality can lead to negative social, economic and political consequences that have a destabilizing effect on societies'; they 'create social and political fractures that can develop into social unrest and insecurity'. Divisions between rich and poor are many and deep and show all the signs of being lasting, as the notorious 'trickle-down' theory helps the rich to stay rich and become richer, but clearly is not working for the benefit of those in poverty. In most places, the effects of rapid economic growth thus far have inextricably linked a fast rise in total and 'average' wealth with an equally fast multiplication of unbearable privations faced by the masses of unemployed and of casual and informal labourers.

For many of us, this may be shocking news, though comfortably muted by distance, as it is reaching us (if at all) from faraway lands. But again, don't say you haven't been warned. What we are talking about here is not just yesterday's peasants crowded in the notoriously sprawling, messy, underfunded, undermanaged and underserviced conurbations of sub-Saharan Africa or Latin America. The United Nations found New York to be the ninth most unequal city in the world, while big and thriving US cities like Atlanta, New Orleans, Washington and Miami are at a level of inequality almost identical with that of Nairobi or Abidjan. Only a few countries, notably Denmark, Finland, the Netherlands and Slovenia, seem to have escaped the universal trend thus far.

In the common view, what is at stake here is inequality of access to education, career tracks and social contacts, and in consequence inequality of material possessions and chances of enjoyment of life. But, as in Göran Therborn's timely reminder, this is not the end of the story, and not even its most conspicuous and consequential part. Aside from 'material' or 'resource' inequality, there is what he calls 'vital inequality'[15] – in different classes and different countries, life expectation and the chance of dying well before achieving adulthood differ sharply: 'A retired British male bank or insurance employee can look forward to seven or eight more years of retirement life than a retired employee of Whitbread or Tesco [supermarket chain].' People at the lowest income level in the official British statistics have four times less chance of reaching retirement at all than people at the top level. Life expectation in the poorest neighbourhood of Glasgow (Calton) is 28 years shorter than in the most privileged area of the same city (Lenzie), or for that matter in the affluent Kensington or Chelsea areas of London. 'Social status hierarchies are, literally, lethal,' Therborn concludes. And there is a third kind or aspect of inequality as well, he adds: 'existential' inequality, one that 'hits you as a person', that 'restricts the freedom of action of certain categories of persons' (for instance, women barred access to public places in Victorian England, but also in many countries today; or Londoners in the East End a hundred years ago, replaced in our time by dwellers in French *banlieues*, Latin American *favelas* or North American urban ghettos). Victims of existential inequality are those categories who have been denied respect, cast as inferior and in the effect humiliated by being stripped of a crucial part of their humanity – like black Americans and Amer-Indians (or 'native nations', as the hypocrisy of political correctness demands them to be called) in the US, poor immigrants, 'low castes' and stigmatized ethnic groups everywhere. The Italian government has recently made existential inequality into a law of the country, and any attempt to soften it a punishable crime: the law now demands that its citizens spy on and report illegal immigrants, and threatens them with prison sentences for helping those people and giving them shelter.

Therborn, along with numerous other observers, has little doubt as to the causes and the morbid consequences of the present explosive rise in human inequality:

> The transformation of capitalist finance into a huge global casino is what has created the current economic crisis, which has put hundreds of thousands out of employment and led to demands for billions of pounds of taxpayers' money. In the South the world crisis is bringing more poverty, hunger and death . . . The stretching social distance between the poorest and the richest diminishes social cohesion, which in turn means more collective problems – such as crime and violence – and fewer resources for solving all our other collective problems, from national identity to climate change.

This is not the end of the story either. Social disturbances, urban unrest, crime, violence, terrorism – these are gruesome enough prospects, portending ill for our security and that of our children. But they are, so to speak, outer symptoms, spectacular and intensely dramatized outbursts of social ills ignited by additions of new humiliations to the old, and developments making inequality that is already deep even deeper. There is another kind of damage left in its track by all that inequality on the rise: moral devastation, ethical blindness and insensitivity, habituation to the sights of human suffering and to the harm done daily by humans to humans – a gradual yet relentless, piecemeal and subterranean to the point of being unnoticed and unresisted, erosion of the values that make life meaningful and human cohabitation feasible and its enjoyment plausible. The late Richard Rorty knew well what was at stake when he appealed to us, his contemporaries:

> We should raise our children to find it intolerable that we who sit behind desks and punch keyboards are paid ten times as much as people who get their hands dirty cleaning our toilets, and a hundred times as much as those who fabricate our keyboards in the Third World. We should ensure that they worry about the fact that the countries which industrialized first have a hundred times the wealth of those who have not yet industrialized. Our children need to learn, early on, to see the inequalities between their own fortunes and those of other children as neither the Will of God nor the necessary price for economic efficiency, but as an evitable tragedy. They should start thinking, as early as possible, about how the world might be changed so as to ensure that no one goes hungry while others have a surfeit.[16]

High time to stop saying that we haven't heard the warnings. Or asking for whom these bells toll, louder by the day.

23

The world inhospitable to education?

(part one)

The 'crisis in education' widely debated nowadays is by no means a novelty. The history of education has been densely spattered with critical periods when it became evident that apparently tested and seemingly reliable premises and strategies were losing their grip on reality, calling for second thoughts, revision and reform. It seems, though, that the present crisis is unlike the crises of the past.

The present-day challenges deliver heavy blows to the very essence of the idea of education as it was formed at the threshold of the long history of civilization. They bring into question the *invariants* of the idea: the constitutive features of education that have withstood all past challenges and emerged unscathed from past crises, assumptions never before looked into or questioned, let alone suspected of having run their course and being in need of replacement.

In the liquid modern world, the solidity of things, much like the solidity of human bonds, tends to be resented as a threat: after all, any oath of allegiance, any long-term (let alone timeless) commitment portends a future burdened with obligations that constrain freedom of movement and reduce the ability to take up new, as yet unknown, chances as they (inevitably) present themselves. The prospect of being saddled with one, intractable thing or bond for the duration of life feels downright repulsive and frightening. And no wonder, since even the most coveted things are known to age fast, to lose their lustre in no time and to turn from a badge of honour into a stigma of shame. The editors of glossy magazines are good at feeling the pulse of time: alongside information about the new 'what you must do' and the new 'what you must have' they regularly supply their readers with advice on 'what is out' and needs to be dumped. Our world is ever more reminiscent of Italo Calvino's 'invisible city' of Leonia where 'it is not so much by the things that are manufactured, sold and bought each day that you can measure opulence . . . but rather by the things that are thrown out each day to make room for the new.'[17] The joy of 'getting rid of', 'putting paid to', discarding and dumping is the true passion of our liquid modern world.

To speak of the ability to last for ever is no longer a term of praise for things or bonds. Things and bonds are expected to serve for only a fixed term, and to be decomposed, shredded or otherwise disposed of once they have outlived their usefulness – which they must do sooner or later. And so possessions, particularly long-lasting possessions one cannot easily get rid of, are to be shunned. Today's consumerism is not about the accumulation of things, but their instantaneous and 'one-off' enjoyment. So why should the 'knowledge package' obtained during a stay at school or college be exempted from that universal rule? In a whirlwind of change, knowledge looks much more attractive when it is fit for instant use and only meant as a 'one-off', the kind of knowledge that boasts of being immediately ready, knowledge for instant disposal of the sort promised by the software programs come on and off the shelves of shops in ever accelerating succession.

And so the thought that education might be a 'product' that is meant to be appropriated and kept for ever and ever is off-putting and most certainly no longer speaks in favour of institutionalized education in schools. To convince their children of the use of learning, fathers and mothers of yore used to tell them that 'what you've learned, no one will ever take away'; that might have been an encouraging promise to their children, but the contemporary young would be horrified if their fathers and mothers still deployed such arguments. Commitments tend to be resented nowadays, unless they come with an 'until further notice' clause. In a growing number of American cities, building permits are only issued with demolition permits, while American generals hotly resist (even though in vain) engaging their troops on the ground unless a convincing 'exit scenario' has been worked out in advance.

The second challenge to the basic premises of education comes from the erratic and essentially unpredictable nature of contemporary change and it adds power to the first challenge. At all times knowledge has been valued for its faithful representation of the world; but what if the world changes in a way that continuously defies the truth of extant knowledge, constantly taking even the 'best informed' people by surprise? Werner Jaeger, the author of a classic exploration of the ancient roots of the concepts of teaching and learning, believed that the idea of education (*Bildung*, 'formation') originally rested on the twin assumptions of an immutable order of the world underlying all the superficial variety of human experience, and of similarly eternal laws governing human nature. The first assumption justified the necessity and benefits of knowledge transmission from teachers to pupils. The second imbued teachers with the kind of self-confidence they needed to insist on the timeless validity of the model they wished their pupils or wards to follow and imitate.

The world we inhabit these days feels on the contrary more like a contraption for forgetting than a setting favouring, and propitious to, learning. Partitions may be impervious and impenetrable, as in that old-style laboratory maze of the behaviourists – but they are on castors and constantly on the move, devaluing as they go the routes tested and explored only yesterday. Woe to people with a retentive memory: yesterday's trusty tracks will be found to end up at blank walls or in quicksand today, and the habitual behavioural patterns, once foolproof, are likely to bring disaster instead of success. In such a world, learning is bound endlessly to chase forever elusive objects, and to make its plight worse the objects would begin to melt the moment they were caught, and since the rewards for proper action tend to be moved to different locations daily, reinforcements would mislead as much as they reassured: they are traps to be wary of and avoid, since they may instil habits and impulses that will prove to be useless in no time, if not downright harmful.

As Ralph Waldo Emerson observed, when you skate on thin ice your salvation is in speed. Salvation-seekers will be well advised to move quickly enough to avoid the risk of overtesting the endurance of any particular spot. In the volatile world of liquid modernity, in which hardly any form keeps its shape long enough to warrant trust and gel into long-term reliability (at any rate, there is no telling when and whether it will gel and little likelihood that it ever will), walking is better than sitting, running is better than walking, and surfing is better still than running. Surfing benefits from the lightness and sprightliness of the surfer; it also helps if the surfers are not too choosy about the waves coming their way and are always ready to cast their former preferences aside.

All that goes against the grain of everything that learning and education stood for through most of their history. After all, they were made to the measure of a world that was durable, was hoped to stay durable and intended to be made still more durable than it had been up to then. In such a world, memory was an asset, and the further back it reached and the longer it lasted the more valuable it was. Today such a solidly entrenched memory seems potentially incapacitating in many cases, misleading in many more, useless in most.

One wonders to what extent the rapid and spectacular career of servers and electronic networks was due to the waste-storage, waste-disposal and waste-recycling problems that servers promised to resolve. With the work of memorizing resulting in more waste than in usable products, and without any reliable way to decide in advance which was which (which of the apparently useful products would soon fall out of fashion and which of the apparently useless ones would enjoy a sudden upsurge of demand), the chance of storing all information in containers kept at a safe distance from brains (where the stored information could and probably would have surreptitiously taken over control of behaviour) was a timely, tempting proposition . . .

(to be continued)

24

The world inhospitable to education?

(part two)

In our volatile world of instant and erratic change, those ultimate objectives of orthodox education such as settled habits, solid cognitive frames and stable value preferences become handicaps. At least they have been cast as such by the knowledge market, to which (as to all markets for all commodities) loyalty, unbreakable bonds and long-term commitments are anathema: they are viewed as so many hindrances to be forced out of the way, and treated accordingly. We have moved from the immutable and frozen maze modelled by behaviourists, and the uniform and monotonous routine modelled by Pavlov, into an open marketplace where anything can happen at any time yet nothing can be done once and for all, and where successful steps are matters of luck and in no way guarantee another success if they are repeated. And the point to remember and appreciate in all its consequences is that in our times the market and the *mappa mundi et vitae* overlap.

As Dany-Robert Dufour has observed, capitalism dreams not only of pushing to the limits of the globe the territory on whose surface every object is a commodity (think of water rights, genome rights, living species, babies, human organs), but also of expanding it downwards to dig up and make available for commercial (profitable) use what were previously private affairs, once left in the charge of the individual (think of subjectivity, sexuality), recycling them into objects of merchandise. And so we all, most of the time and whatever our momentary preoccupations, share the plight of Konrad Lorenz's laboratory sticklebacks exposed to conflicting and confusing signals. The bizarre behaviour of the male sticklebacks, unsure of the boundaries separating contradictory behavioural patterns, is fast turning into the most common conduct of male and female human beings. Responses tend to be as confused as the signals are confusing.

The trouble is that little, if anything, can be done about all that by a reform of educational strategies alone, however ingenious, elaborate and thorough it may be. Neither the commonality of the stickleback's plight nor the sudden attraction of Don Giovanni's life strategy (of finishing quickly and starting from scratch) can be laid at the door of educators and blamed on their faults or neglect alone. It is the world *outside* the school buildings that has grown quite different from the kind of world for which classical schools, as described for instance by Jaeger, used to prepare their students.

In this new world, humans are expected to seek private solutions to socially generated troubles, instead of looking for socially generated solutions to private troubles. During the 'solid' phase of modern history, let me repeat, the setting for human actions was construed or forced, expected and wished to emulate, as far as possible, the pattern of the behaviourists' maze, in which the distinction between right and wrong itineraries was clear-cut and permanent, so that those who missed or abandoned the right track were invariably punished on the spot, while those who followed it obediently and staunchly were rewarded. Massive Fordist factories and mass conscription armies, the two longest arms of solid modern panoptical power, were the fullest embodiments of that tendency towards the strict routinization of stimuli and responses. 'Domination' consisted in the right to set unbreakable rules, supervise their implementation, put those who were bound to follow the rules under continuous surveillance and bring deviants back into line, or expel them if the effort to reform them failed. That pattern of domination required a constant mutual co-presence and mutual engagement of the managers and the managed. In every panoptical structure there was a Pavlov who determined the sequence of moves and saw to it that it repeated itself monotonously, immune to any present or future counterpressures. With the designers and supervisors of the Panopticon guaranteeing the durability of settings and the repetitiveness of situations and choices, it paid to learn the rules by heart and gel them into habits that were solidly set, deeply ingrained and hence invariably followed. 'Solid' modernity was an era closely approximated to such all-embracing, rigidly managed and tightly supervised, durable settings.

In our 'liquid' stage of modernity, however, demand is fast drying up for such orthodox managerial functions. Domination can be gained and assured with much less expenditure of effort, time and money, through a threat by managers to disengage or refuse to engage, rather than by obtrusive control and surveillance. The threat of disengagement shifts the burden of proof, the generation and maintenance of a liveable arrangement, onto the other, the dominated, side. It is now up to subordinates to behave in a way likely to find favour in the bosses' eyes and entice them to 'buy' their services and their individually designed 'products' – just as the producers and traders of other goods seduce prospective customers to desire the commodities they put on sale. 'Following a routine' would not suffice to achieve that purpose. As Luc Boltanski and Eve Chiapello found, anyone who wants to succeed in the arrangement that has replaced the 'rat maze' kind of employment setting needs to demonstrate conviviality and communicative skills, openness and curiosity – offering for sale their own person, their whole person, as a unique and irreplaceable value that will enhance the quality of the team.[18] It is now up to current or would-be employees to 'monitor themselves', to be their own observers, in order to make sure that their performance is convincing and likely to be approved by their purchasers – and likely to go on being approved in the event that the desires, appetites and taste of the buyers change. It is no longer up to their bosses to blunt and polish any sharp or rough edges of the personality and otherwise smother the idiosyncrasies of their employees, homogenize their conduct and lock their actions into a stiff frame of routine, thereby making them into a purchasable commodity.

The recipe for success is 'to be oneself' and not 'like all the rest'. It is difference, not sameness, that sells best. It is no longer enough to have the knowledge and skills 'ascribed to the job' and already demonstrated by others who did the work before or are currently applying for it; most likely, this will be seen and treated as a disadvantage. What is needed instead are unusual ideas 'unlike any other', exceptional projects no one has suggested before, and above all a cat-like inclination to walk one's own solitary way.

This is the kind of knowledge (inspiration rather) coveted by men and women of liquid modern times. They want counsellors who show them how to walk, rather than teachers who make sure that only one road – an already overcrowded road because it is the 'one and only' – is taken. The counsellors they want, and for whose services they are ready to pay as much as it takes, are supposed to (and will) help them to dig into the depths of their character and personality, where the rich deposits of precious ore are presumed to lie, clamouring for excavation. The counsellors will probably reproach their clients for sloth or negligence, rather than ignorance; they will proffer a 'how to' kind of knowledge, *savoir être* or *vivre*, rather than the *savoir*, 'know that' kind of knowledge which orthodox educators wished to impart and were good at transmitting to their pupils.

The current cult of 'lifelong education' is focused partly on the need to update professional information to the 'state of the art'. Yet in an equal, perhaps greater, part it owes its popularity to the conviction that the mine of personality is never exhausted and that spiritual masters are still to be found who know how to reach the as yet unexploited or even undiscovered deposits which other guides could not reach or abominably overlooked – and that those masters will be found with due effort. And of course with arms and legs available in sufficient quantity to pay for their services.

(to be continued)

25

The world inhospitable to education?

(part three)

The triumphant march of knowledge through the world inhabited by modern men and women proceeded on two fronts.

On the first, new and as yet unexplored parts or aspects of the world were invaded, captured, scrutinized and mapped. The empire built thanks to advances on the first front was that of information meant to represent the world: at the moment of representation, the represented part of the world was assumed to have been 'made intelligible': conquered and claimed for human beings.

The second front was that of education: it progressed by expanding the canon of education and stretching the perceptive and retentive capacities of the educated.

On both fronts, the 'finishing line' of the advance – the end of the war – was clearly visualized from the start: all blank spots would eventually be filled in, a complete *mappa mundi* would be drawn, and thus all the information necessary and sufficient to move freely through the world would be made available to members of the human species through the provision of the number of educational transmission channels that was needed. The trouble, however, was that the further the war progressed and the longer the list of victorious battles grew, the further away the 'finishing line' seemed to recede . . .

We are inclined now to believe that the war remains as unwinnable as it was from the start, and on both fronts. To begin with, the mapping of each freshly conquered territory seems to increase rather than diminish the size and number of blank spots, and so the moment when a *compleat mappa mundi* can be drawn seems no more imminent. To continue, the world 'out there', the world it was once hoped to incarcerate and immobilize in an act of representation, now seems to slip swiftly and nimbly away from every recorded shape; it is a player (and a shrewd, crafty and cunning player, to be sure) in the game of truth, rather than being the stake and the prize human players hoped to win and share. In Paul Virilio's succinct yet vivid summary, today's world no longer has any kind of stability; it shifts, straddles and glides away all the time.

Even more seminal news comes from the second, educational front, however, the distribution of knowledge. To follow Virilio once more, the unknown has shifted its position: from the world, which was far too vast, mysterious and savage, into the nebular galaxy of the image. Explorers willing to examine that galaxy in its entirety are few and far between, and those able to do so are even fewer. Scientists, artists and philosophers alike find themselves in a kind of new alliance for the exploration of that galaxy – a kind of alliance which ordinary people may as well abandon all hope of ever joining. That particular galaxy is, purely and simply, unassimilable. It is not so much the world of which the information tells, but the information itself that has now turned into the prime site of the 'unknown'. It is information that feels far too vast, mysterious and savage. It seems to recycle itself from being a royal road to knowing the world into a major barrier to that knowledge. The gigantic volumes of information vying for attention are felt by ordinary men and women nowadays to be considerably more bewildering, off-putting, and menacing than the few remaining 'mysteries of the universe', of interest solely to a small bunch of science addicts and an even smaller handful of Nobel Prize contenders.

All things unknown feel menacing, but they prompt different reactions. The blank spots on the map of the universe arouse curiosity, spur to action and give determination, courage and confidence to the adventurous. They promise an interesting and adventurous life of discovery; they augur a better future gradually freed from the nuisances poisoning life. It is different, though, in the case of the impenetrable and impervious mass of information: it is all here, available and within reach, yet it tauntingly, infuriatingly evades the daring effort to pierce through it, digest and assimile it.

It is the mass of accumulated knowledge that has become the contemporary epitome of disorder and chaos. In that mass, in the manner of the mysterious cosmic black holes, all orthodox ordering devices – topics of relevance, the assignment of importance, needs determining usefulness and authorities determining value – have been progressively sunk, swallowed and dissolved. The mass makes its contents look uniformly colourless. In that mass, one may say, all pieces of information flow with the same specific gravity, and for people who are denied the right to claim expertise for their own judgements but are buffeted by the cross-currents of contradictory expert claims, there is no evident, let alone fool-proof, way to sift the wheat from the chaff. In that mass, parcels of knowledge carved out for consumption and personal use can be evaluated only by their quantity; there is no chance of comparing their quality with that of other parcels in the mass. One bit of information equals another. TV quizzes faithfully reflect that new condition of human knowledge: every right answer has the same number of points awarded to the contestant, regardless of the topic of the question and its 'specific gravity' (how could one measure that gravity anyway?!).

Assigning importance to various bits of information, and in the process, assigning more importance to some than to others, is perhaps the most perplexing task and the most difficult decision to take. The sole rule of thumb to be guided by is momentary topical relevance; but then the relevance shifts in the next moment and the assimilated bits lose their significance as soon as they have been mastered. Like other commodities in the market, they are for instant, on-the-spot and 'one-off' use.

Time for a conclusion . . .

Education took many forms in the past and proved itself able to adjust to changing circumstances, setting itself new goals and designing new strategies. But let me repeat – the present change is not like past changes. At no turning-point in human history did educators face a challenge strictly comparable to the one presented by the current watershed. Simply, we have never been in such a situation before. The art of living in a world oversaturated with information has still to be learned. And so has the yet more mind-bogglingly difficult art of grooming human beings for such a life.

26

Ghosts of New Years past and New Years to come

New Year? What do we celebrate on New Year's Eve, on the new year's first day, and particularly at the magic moment that separates them, that midnight like no other midnight in that year just ended (the memory is fresh) and (so we expect) in this year just starting? A baffling question, if you think about it: after all, those two winter days, 31 December and 1 January, are strikingly similar, hardly distinguishable – 24 hours or 1,440 minutes in each, and separated by a distance not a second longer than that separating any other two consecutive days. Neither are they dates like the winter solstice, when the night starts its annual retreat and days once more promise to be longer . . .

What indeed is there to celebrate on this particular day? Nothing else, it seems, except a sense of accomplishing something we felt the need to accomplish, a sense we have invested at random in this, rather than in any other day: a sense of closing one chapter and opening another, perhaps completely different chapter. A sense of putting paid to old troubles and worries, troubles and worries past, and so too solid now to be dabbled with and fit only for burial or oblivion; and (if we try hard enough, as we would like to and are hoping to) also a sense of taking off to a time unlike times past, a new time, a different time – a future still soft, flexible, kneadable and obedient to our will, a time in which nothing has yet been lost and everything is still to be gained. Perhaps a time free of the troubles we knew and the worries we went through. In short, a start to 'something completely different'. At that magic moment separating the last second of the 'old year' and the first of the 'new' we celebrate the *possibility* of *cutting our losses* and *starting again*, from the beginning, in a way that will allow us to leave unwanted ballast behind, once and for all; the possibility of making the past (about which nothing can be done) fully and truly *past*, and the future fully and truly a *future* (in which everything is possible).

At New Year we *celebrate our hopes*. And more than any other of the many hopes we cherish, the 'meta-hope', the 'mother of all hopes': the hope that, this time at last, unlike in past trials and tribulations, our hopes won't be frustrated and dashed, and our resolve to fulfil them won't prematurely wilt, flag and run out of vigour, as our hopes and resolutions did in the past. New Year is the annual festivity marking *the resurrection of hopes*. We dance, sing and drink to welcome the arrival of the born-again, as yet uncompromised *hope*; a hope, as we hope, of a new kind – a kind immune to being discredited and disparaged . . .

In Britain people are trained from early childhood to make 'New Year resolutions', regularly, year in, year out. Most of us, here in Britain, persist in making them year in, year out, long into our lives, sometimes till the very end. The resolutions may be of all sorts, though most of them tend to be concerned with cutting out something bad and unpleasant and replacing it with something better and more enticing: they may signal our wish to stop smoking or take up regular physical exercise, to put a personal relationship straight or finish it off, to start saving instead of wasting money, to pay elderly parents more frequent visits instead of hanging up early when they call, to pay more attention to our career or study and work harder at it, instead of keeping it on a side burner, to finally repaint the flaking ceiling in the kitchen, to be kinder, more understanding and caring to our partner, to friends, or children . . . New Year resolutions tend to be about *becoming a better sort of person*; better for others, and better for oneself: about acquiring (and deserving) more respect.

It would be nice – deeply satisfying – to persist in fulfilling these resolutions long enough to finish the wished/intended/planned/promised oneself job, or make the improvements in character last longer than the first few January days. Alas, all too often our good intentions are not matched by the strength of our will. The custom of repeating the act of making resolutions *annually* (instead of practising the art of making tough resolutions and holding to them day in, day out) does not help. If I fail to fulfil my New Year resolution, everything is not lost, this stain can be – will be – wiped out; there will be another New Year, another chance, another occasion to draw a line and start again, and there is still plenty of time to gather strength and build stamina to ensure the success of that next attempt. A new start means new challenges, but challenges can wait (be ignored or put on a shelf) until the next occasion arrives to earnestly confront them point blank, another New Year's Day, that is. But let us observe that getting used to comforting our consciences in such a way is a mixed blessing: flaking ceilings can perhaps wait another year for a fresh layer of paint, parents will probably forgive their children once more for their insufficient attention, even smoking for another year won't necessarily kill us just like that – but there are things that shout out for our determined action and cannot wait long; there are acts which we can delay only at our joint peril; and there are tasks which, if not attended to right away, may grow too big and too intractable for us to handle.

I believe you know what I mean; it is really impossible *not* to know, as we approach the end of the first decade of a century in which the fate of humanity, now inextricably linked with the fate of all other living creatures (innocent 'collateral victims' of our collective self-indulgence, overgrown self-confidence and underdeveloped sense of responsibility), is at stake. We – all of us, humans – are nearing, and fast, a few or more inches closer with each successive year, the edge of a precipice. A catastrophe as enormous, as gruesome, as that other overheating of the planet, the one that happened around 250 million years ago, destroying 95 per cent of living species and leaving the future of the rest hanging on an exceptionally thin thread for the next couple of thousand years.

That past catastrophe, unlike the one we are now watching come nearer while doing next to nothing to stop it or at least slow down a bit, was triggered by a volcanic explosion emitting trillions of tons of carbon dioxide that pushed up the temperature of the earth by 5 degrees, which in turn meant that huge volumes of methane, a gas 25 times more powerful than carbon dioxide, were shaken out of the unstable compounds covering the bottom of the ocean – and released into the atmosphere, to push up the temperature by a further 5 degrees . . . A chain reaction: once it had started and reached a critical point, it could not be arrested. The point is, though, that for a restaging of a catastrophe of that sort in the coming years, we (if any 'we' are left to apportion the guilt, that is) won't be able to blame the vagaries of nature, contingencies which, despite all our skills and ingenuity, we, human beings, could not prevent. The next production of the drama may well be the outcome of *our own* disastrous, and in the end suicidal, way of using and abusing the planet we inhabit, and we (if there are any 'we' left to make excuses, that is) won't even be able to apologize by saying that such an outcome was 'not anticipated'. No one can say today that she or he does not know what sort of a future is brewing. Or why it is brewing. Or what she or he, and all the rest of us, *ought* to do, and what we all *must* stop doing immediately if we really wish to stand even a modest chance of averting the disaster. Everyone knows what our resolutions should contain – and everyone knows that it is the last moment to make them and stick to them through thick and thin. Whatever the cost to our comfort and whatever sacrifice might be demanded from us for holding to our resolution.

These are my New Year wishes to you, to my and your children, and to my and your children's children. And to myself.

27

Predicting the unpredictable

On a Tuesday some weeks ago I was going to travel to Rome for a lecture. I wished to know what weather to expect – how to dress for the trip. I checked the weather forecast on the preceding Friday. There will be heavy rains in Rome, it said, and temperatures up to 15 degrees. Just in case, I rechecked the forecast on Monday. It predicted quite a different picture for the same day: cloudless sky and temperatures falling below 12 degrees . . . What the weather in Rome actually turned out to be on Tuesday was something I could not check personally, because my flight was cancelled due to a sudden snowstorm which caught the airport staff completely unprepared . . .

In the early 1960s, Edward Lorenz worked on a program that would allow forthcoming changes of weather to be predicted more precisely. To the unanimous admiration and selective envy of his colleagues, he was coming quite close to a comprehensive and well-nigh foolproof model of the weather forecast, with all factors taken into account. One day, though, he restarted work in his laboratory to find to his great astonishment, that slightly altering just one of the many initial variables (rounding up its quantity to a thousandth) resulted in the same program turning out a widely (one is tempted to say: wildly!) different prediction. A minute, trifling, negligible difference in just one variable, by an amount that sometimes eluded even the most precise measurements, and so was usually ignored, could have profound effects on the outcome of the whole system. The smallest difference could grow in the course of time to gigantic, indeed catastrophic, proportions. A butterfly flapping its wings in Beijing, as Lorenz himself put it, could affect the formation and itinerary of hurricanes in the Gulf of Mexico, many months later and thousands of miles away.

This capacity for the consequences of minuscule changes to swell at an exponential rate is now known by the name of the 'butterfly effect'. The rule of the butterfly effect says bluntly that the behaviour of complex systems with a number of mutually independent variables is and will forever remain, to put it in a nutshell, *unpredictable*. Not just unpredictable *to us*, because of ignorance, negligence or dim-headedness, but by their, the systems', very nature. Because the world we inhabit is as complex a system as can be imagined, its *future is a great unknown*; and it is bound to remain unknown whatever we do. Predictions can only be guesses, and trusting them means taking a huge risk. The future is unpredictable because it is, purely and simply, *undetermined*. At any moment, there is more than one road the future course of events can take . . .

And yet . . . Trying hard to defy that indomitable obstacle and wrench out of the future an advance copy of its likeness, force it to reveal itself in advance, when it is still merely pending (indeed, not yet born) – in short, to obtain a portrait of an as-yet-unexisting sitter – is precisely what humans have earnestly tried to do and hoped to achieve since the dawn of history: millennia before meteorology, following the example of modern science, set about the serious business of finding the precise laws that determine the twists and turns of nature, history and human fate, so they could be predicted: so it could be known what the future would be like, and known *now, before* that future turns itself into another present. Aeromancy, alectoromancy, aleuromancy, alphitomancy, anthropomancy, anthroposcopy, arithmancy, astro-diagnosis, astrognosy, astrology, astromancy, austromancy, axino-mancy . . . these are the names of the ancient methods to divine the future, and only those of them that start with the letter 'A' (and there are so many letters in the alphabet!). They were all practised by widely and deeply respected sages of the past, and deeply trusted by many people who admired the soothsayers' and oracles' visible self-confidence and apparent skills. They have been all discredited and by and large discarded, or downright forgotten, these days. One wonders whether meteorology will join their ranks sometime in the future . . .

By now we are used to the vagaries of notoriously capricious climes; we do not normally make a tragedy of this common, almost daily inconvenience. There are, though, much more serious, disturbing and worrying affairs at stake in the risky business of predicting the future: the most seminal events of the last century took our fathers and grandfathers by surprise and caught them unprepared. No one managed to predict the spectacular rise and spread of cruel authoritarian and dictatorial regimes, let alone their 'new and improved', totalitarian variety. A few dozen years later, the 'science of Sovietology' – a branch of scholarship now deceased and happily buried, but then permanently and lavishly awash with funds, armed with numerous research institutes and boasting thousands of celebrated scholars – on the very eve of the collapse of the Berlin Wall was still split between luminaries predicting a gradual, but unrelenting 'convergence' between capitalist and socialist systems in the form of so-called 'corporatism' (now a largely forgotten term, no longer part of the vocabulary of respectable scholarship), and boffins who predicted the conflict between them would get inflamed and lead to a devastating (possibly nuclear) explosion, MAD (mutually assured destruction) style; not a single respectable gathering of sovietology experts seriously broached the *implosion* of the Soviet system under the burden of its own inanity – just as the present earthquake in the consumer-led and credit-operated economy, its suddenness, depth, spread and resistance to habitually applied remedial measures was not anticipated by any world congress of economists . . . In both these cases, the number of correct predictions fell well below the proportion of right answers to be expected by the laws of probability in a large set of random guesses. Even now, wiser after the event, we are desperately seeking the fatal 'butterfly' whose flapping wing was responsible for this devastating 'effect', whose consequences still defy all prognoses!

Vaclav Havel – indefatigable dissenter and freedom warrior and, many battles later, the President of the Czech Republic, a man who spent his life on the frontline of history trying not just to anticipate the future but to make sure that it took and kept to a humane and human-friendly direction – summarized his experience by saying that in order to know what turn the future would take, one needs to know what songs people are currently singing; but the snag is, he added right away, that there is no knowing what songs people will be singing next year, yet alone the year after . . . In the complex system called 'history', human conduct is by far the most variable of variables; and the least predictable among unpredictables.

In our vocabulary we human beings have a little word 'no', which enables us to question, deny or reject the 'facts of the matter' and 'the state of affairs' we are presented with by the world we live in. In our grammar we have the future tense, which enables us to imagine and visualize a state of affairs different from that presently existing – a 'matter' with quite different 'facts'. Armed with such weapons, we are bound to be underdetermined and therefore free, but also doomed to make choices, exposed to the constant danger of choosing wrongly and condemned to perpetual uncertainty. Insecurity about the present and uncertainty about the future are our constant companions in our journey through life. No wonder we dream of a telephone line to, or an internet address of someone we would once have called a 'prophet', 'oracle' or 'soothsayer', but nowadays prefer to call an 'expert', someone hovering at a height from which – in the absence of angels – only birds view this world of ours, and so someone who is able to tell us in advance what she or he sees, round the next corner, in that future inaccessible to our own eyes, fixed on ground level. But then, let me repeat, no bird can scan the future, because the future, as long as it remains a future, does not exist, and so there is nothing for even the sharpest and most conveniently located eye to see. The 'future' is just a shorthand expression for 'anything might happen, but nothing can be known or done for sure'; ironically, however, we, inveterate human choosers, are the ones who make those future happenings happen. It is human nature to go on asking questions about the shape of the future, while making reliable answers (as distinct from merely credible, and so uncertain, guesses) impossible to achieve courtesy of our freedom of choice.

It was the great Italian Antonio Gramsci who insisted that the only way of 'predicting' the future was to join forces and pool our efforts in order to cause future events to conform to what we desire, and to steer clear from undesirable scenarios. There is no guarantee that these efforts will bring the result we wish to achieve; the *war* against uncertainty will never be comprehensively won. But this is the sole strategy that gives us a chance of winning *battles*. Not the perfect solution, but the only one available. Take it or leave it.

28
Calculating the incalculable

Risk, says Ulrich Beck, the pioneer of contemporary explorations of the subject and still its leading and by far its most proficient theorist, has from the beginning of modernity 'amalgamate[d] knowledge with non-knowing within the semantic horizon of probability'.[19] 'The history of science dates the birth of probability calculus, the first attempt to bring the unpredictable under control – developed in correspondence between Pierre Fermat and Blaise Pascal – to the year 1651'. Since then, through the category of risk, Beck adds, 'the arrogant assumption of controllability' can increase its influence.

From our perspective in the clearly liquidized sequel to the compulsively liquidizing yet solidity-obsessed stage of early modernity (and so with the benefit of hindsight), we can say that the category of risk was an attempt to reconcile the two pillars of modern consciousness: an awareness of the contingency and randomness of the world, on the one hand, and a 'we can' type of self-confidence (Beck prefers to call it 'arrogance'), on the other. More exactly, the category of 'risk' was an attempt to salvage the second pillar, despite the insistent and ubiquitous, even though resented and feared, company of the first. The category of 'risk' (and the ensuing project of 'calculating risk') promised that even though the natural world and the additions and alterations made by human beings were bound to fall well short of unconditional regularity, and so of the ideal of a genuinely complete and reliable predictability, gathering and storing knowledge while flexing its practical, technological arm might still bring humans quite close to the condition of certainty or at least of a high probability of prognosticating correctly – and thus of 'being in control'. The category of 'risk' did not promise foolproof security from danger: but it promised the ability to *calculate the probability of danger and its likely volume* – and so, obliquely, the possibility of calculating and applying the best distribution of resources to render intended undertakings maximally effective and successful.

Even if not explicitly, the semantics of 'risk' needed to assume, axiomatically, a 'second best' universe: a 'structured' ('structuring': the manipulation, skewing or slanting, and thereby differentiating, of an otherwise random distribution of probabilities), or in other words an essentially rule-abiding environment – a universe in which, if not the *occurrence* of events, then at least the *probabilities* of their occurrence are predetermined, and can be scrutinized, made known and assessed. But however far short the 'calculation of risk' may stop from a flawless and infallible certainty, and thus from the prospect of predetermining the future, that distance will seem small and insignificant in comparison with the unbridgeable categorial abyss separating the 'semantic horizon of probability' (and so also the feasibility of the hoped-for calculation of risk) from the land salvaged from that haunting and daunting premonition of irremovable and irreparable uncertainty which hovers over our present, liquid modern consciousness.

As John Gray pointed out a dozen years ago, 'the governments of sovereign states do not know in advance how markets will react . . . National governments in the 1990s are flying blind.' Gray does not expect the future to usher us into a markedly different condition; as in the past, we can expect 'a succession of contingencies, catastrophes and occasional lapses into peace and civilization'[20] – all of them, let me add, unexpected, unforeseeable and incalculable in advance, more often than not catching their victims as well as their beneficiaries by surprise, unaware and unprepared.

It seems ever more likely that the discovery and announcement of the centrality of the 'risk horizon' in modern thinking shared the eternal habit of the Owl of Minerva, which spread its wings at the end of the day and just before nightfall; or the yet more common proclivity of objects, noted by Martin Heidegger, to be transported from 'hiding in the light' (staying immersed in the obscure condition of *zuhanden*, too obvious to note – or, to use Jose Saramago's description from his *Memorial do convento* of 1982, because they are 'so common, and call for so little skill, that they tend to be overlooked') to the dazzling visibility of the *vorhanden*, of 'problems' to be 'faced up to' and 'resolved' now before going bust, breaking out of the taken for granted, or otherwise frustrating the (as a rule, only half-conscious and tacit) expectations of their habitual users. In other words, things 'burst into consciousness' and become known thanks to their disappearance or an unprecedented, and thus shocking, change. Indeed, we have only become acutely conscious of the awesome roles played by the categories of 'risk', 'risk calculation' and 'risk taking' in our modern history at the moment when the term 'risk' has lost much of its former utility and can only be used (as Jacques Derrida would suggest) *sous rature*, 'under erasure', having turned (to use Beck's own vocabulary) into a 'zombie concept'. When, in other words, the time has arrived to replace the concept of *Risikogesellschaft* – the risk society – with that of *Unsicherheitglobalschaft* – the uncertainty globe.

Our present dangers differ from those the category of 'risk' strove to capture and bring to light because they are *unnamed* until they strike, *unpredictable* and *incalculable*. And the setting for the birth of our dangers, from which they emerge, is no longer framed by the *Gesellschaft* or society – unless the concept of *Gesellschaft*, in opposition to its orthodox connotations, is made coterminous not with the population of a territorial nation-state, but with the *population of the planet*, with humanity as a whole.

The power that matters (that is, power that has, if not the final say, then at least a paramount influence on the set of options open to agents' choices) is growing in volume and has already turned global; politics, however, has remained as local as before. Accordingly, the presently most relevant power stays beyond the reach of the existing political institutions, whereas the framework for manoeuvre in politics within the state continues to shrink. The state of affairs on the planet is now buffeted by ad hoc alliances or just assemblies of discordant powers, unconstrained by political control because of the increasing powerlessness of the political institutions currently available. The latter are thus forced to limit their ambitions severely and to 'hive off', 'outsource' or 'contract out' to non-political agencies a growing number of the functions traditionally entrusted to the governance of national governments. The emaciation of the political sphere (in its institutionalized, orthodox meaning) is self-propelling, as the loss of relevance of successive segments of national politics rebounds in the erosion of citizens' interest in institutionalized politics, and in a widespread tendency to replace it with a drive to experiment with 'free-floating' and electronically mediated quasi/inchoate/incipient politics; a kind of politics distinguished by its expeditiousness, but also noted for being ad hoc, short-termist, confined to single issues, fragile and staunchly resistant, or perhaps even immune, to institutionalization (all those qualities being known to be mutually dependent as well as mutually sustaining and reinforcing).

Since the present-day uncertainty is rooted in global space, the task of restoring the lost balance between power and politics can be performed only at the global level, and only by (alas not yet existing) global lawmaking supported by executive and juridical institutions. This challenge translates into a requirement to complement a hitherto almost wholly 'negative' globalization (that is, the globalization of forces intrinsically hostile to institutionalized politics, such as capital, finance, commodity trade, information, criminality, traffic in drugs and arms, etc.) by its 'positive' counterpart (the globalization of political representation, law and jurisdiction, for instance), which has not yet started in earnest.

The dangers looming in the void extending between the vastness of human interdependency and the narrowness of the tools of human self-government are, in stark opposition to the ideal type of risk, neither predictable and calculable, nor for that reason manageable. Making them so is a task still outstanding; coping with that task will provide the history of the current century with most of its impetus and content.

29

Phobia's twisted trajectories

Phobia (a 'fear of . . .') is a condition akin to dread and horror, but one that also includes an enhanced sensitivity, aversion or allergy focused on some specific sensations: certain kinds of images, sounds, smells, tastes – and so, obliquely, certain kinds of people, animals, substances or situations held responsible for producing these distasteful, off-putting, wicked and repellent sensual impressions. We suspect that coming into contact with these causes of phobia, the carriers of resented phobic effects and/or the entities or substances guilty of perpetrating them might have morbid consequences for us – or that's what we fear, at any rate; and so we try to avoid coming close to them, into visual, auditory, olfactory and particularly tactile contact, at all costs. Phobias nudge us into keeping our distance and erecting impenetrable walls, weaving dense barbed-wire entanglements or digging unbridgeable moats – everything it is hoped will prevent the offending things from leaking, seeping or percolating anywhere close to our living space.

In short, we develop a phobia when we feel afraid, focusing our dreads on specific things we believe to be the culprits, and taking defensive measures to keep those things at a distance. That much is clear. Whether those things would really do us the kind of harm we suspect them of delivering is less clear; even less clear is the causal connection between them and the pains we suffer. It may be that our complaint is altogether unjustified, because the genuine causes of our anxiety lie elsewhere; and that keeping the assumed offenders out of reach won't do much to placate, let alone chase away, our sense of menace. Paradoxically, it is the actions we undertake to save us from the torments of fear that may well turn out to be the most prolific and steady source of those fears . . .

The probability that this will happen rises in parallel with the eminent vagueness and elusiveness of our present-day anxieties. Indeed, everything in our lives may seem to be OK: there is enough money in my bank account, my boss gives me a friendly smile while he lavishly praises my latest project, my partner declares and shows love and devotion, likes to touch me and be touched by me, my kids keep bringing home good marks from the school; why do I worry, then? Why do the days seem dark instead of bright? Whence my discomfort? Why can't I sleep quietly and restfully through the night and why do I wake up full of sinister premonitions? Why can't I just go on and keep smiling?!

To think of it, that 'why' is not so baffling after all. My bank account is in the black as long as I hold on to my job, but each time I open the newspaper I read about new cuts and new redundancies, and so I can't feel secure, and I can't know how long this blissful state will last, I can't be sure that tomorrow there will still be a job to hold on to. My boss poured praise on my latest project, but for how long is a success likely to be remembered and permit me to bask in its glory? Will it be remembered when it comes to another round of mergers or rationalizations or outsourcing and contracting out, as it surely must, sooner rather than later? I and my partner both seem to get satisfaction from our partnership, but what if my partner is the first to decide that enough is enough, that whatever pleasure was there to be creamed off our togetherness already has been, and that the time has arrived to move on? The kids have steered clear of trouble thus far, but how long will it be before they fall into bad company, succumb to drug pushers or fail to avoid child molesters' traps? All that is horrifying enough, but if only this was the end of the list of worries . . . Well, the list is anything but finished – and can it ever be finished?

As Roberto Toscano, Italian diplomat and acute analyst of the contemporary global scene, points out, 'there are few doubts about the gravity of the present crisis, characterized by a lethal combination of economic downturn, widespread political instability, new questions on the vitality of democratic systems, terrorism, the radicalisation of communal identities often turning to violence, the ominous threats to the very survival of the earth.' And then that other factor, perhaps no less potent than all the those – a factor noted recently by the Italian sociologist Ilvo Diamanti: 'The fear Italians feel has little to do with reality. That fear is operated by the TV pilot'. Indeed, when the level of criminality recorded in Italy was falling before the last election, TV channels owned and managed by the Berlusconi family, beefed up day after day the horror of criminals round every corner and under every bed. That happened in Italy. But hardly in Italy alone . . .

There are many things lacking or in short supply in this world of ours, but credible reasons to expect trouble are surely not among them. It is only natural that we all, to one extent or another, suffer from *phobophobia* (a term coined recently by Harmon Leon) – a phobia of phobias, fear of fears. It is the fear of being afraid that haunts us, the denizens of the liquid modern, fast-moving, foggy and messy, unpredictable world teeming with snares and pitfalls.

The fear of being frightened, and frightened with an all-too-valid reason – frightened by a menace still elusive, imprecise and not to be pinpointed, but certain to reveal its whole Gorgon-like face, its fully and truly horrifying countenance and hellish force once it comes out of the darkness where it is currently hiding – this is the most common and the most harrowing of the phobias specific to our century. The hard core of that phobia is the prospect of finding ourselves abandoned and alone at the moment of misfortune. The most common and most avidly sought and widely applied preventive medicine against that happening is the effort to seek shelter in the company of other potential sufferers from the phobia, just like ourselves: holding hands and not letting them go, *keeping in touch, staying in touch and never falling out of touch* – the effort in which most of us invest more zeal and energy, most of the time, than in any other of our innumerable routine undertakings.

Remember the 1999 film *The Blair Witch Project* that announced the advent of the 'stay in touch, or perish' century? The horror that descended on, incapacitated and in the end devoured the three young heroes of that chilling story boiled down, – so far as their viewers could see – to flat batteries in their mobiles and having wandered beyond the reach of the network's coverage. You can easily imagine that kind of horror, because most of us have felt its bitter, pungent taste, at one time or another, even if, thank God, in a diluted and attenuated version: when, for instance, we have left our mobile at home, neglected to recharge the battery, lost it or had it stolen (people have been heard confessing that going out without a mobile makes them feel they are walking down the street without any trousers: naked and defenceless, and doubly humiliated – by mortifying shame and the inability to do anything about it).

I guess what is primarily at stake is not so much the *being in touch* as the making sure again and again that one *can get in touch* right away, whenever the need or wish arises. Do you often resist interrupting a face-to-face meeting with a friend in order to answer your mobile promptly as it brutally, obtrusively rings or vibrates for your attention? Does not the length of the Facebook roll-call of addresses available for voice or text messages feel more satisfying than actually talking or listening to one of their owners? And is not the most endearing and seductive virtue of that latest contraption, 'twittering', the chance it offers of making your presence known to, and felt by, huge numbers of people – numbers far exceeding your capacity, or willingness, for a meaningful conversation?

Exclusion, eviction, being left alone, finding oneself abandoned, cast out or blacklisted or otherwise banished, falling behind or overboard, being refused admission, ignored, kept waiting and made to feel uninvited: these are the most common nightmares in this world of ours, known as it is for its massive production of surpluses and redundancies.

Interregnum

Sometime in the late 1920s or early 1930s Antonio Gramsci recorded in one of the many notebooks he filled during his long incarceration in the prison in Turi di Bari: 'The crisis consists precisely in the fact that the old is dying and the new cannot be born; in this interregnum a great variety of morbid symptoms appear.'[21]

The term 'interregnum' was originally used to denote a time gap separating the death of one royal sovereign from the enthronement of a successor, those intervals being the main occasions on which past generations experienced (and customarily expected) a rupture in the otherwise dull, monotonous continuity of government, law and social order. Ancient Roman law put an official stamp on this understanding of the term (and its referent) by accompanying *interregnum* with the proclamation of *justitium*, that is (as Giorgio Agamben reminded us in his 2003 study *Lo stato di eccezione*) a transition period during which the laws that were binding under the deceased emperor are suspended (admittedly temporarily), presumably in anticipation that new and different laws would be proclaimed by the new sovereign. Gramsci infused the concept of 'interregnum' with a new meaning, however, embracing a wider section of the socio-political-legal order while simultaneously reaching deeper into the socio-cultural realities underlying it. Or rather (taking a leaf from Lenin's memorable definition of a 'revolutionary situation' as a condition in which the rulers no longer *can* rule in their old ways, while the ruled no longer *wish* to be so ruled), Gramsci detached the idea of 'interregnum' from its time-hallowed association with an interlude in a *routine* transmission of hereditary or elected power. He attached it instead to *extraordinary* situations: to times when the extant legal frame of social order loses its grip and can no longer keep burgeoning social life on track, and a new frame, made to the measure of the newly emerged conditions responsible for making the old frame useless, is still at the design stage, has not yet been fully assembled, or has not been made strong enough to be enforced and settled in place.

It can be said, following a recent suggestion by Keith Tester,[22] that the present-day condition of the planet bears many a mark of another interregnum. Indeed, just as Gramsci postulated, 'the old is dying'. The old order, founded on the close association, intertwining or blending (indeed a virtual unity) of territory, state and nation, and on power wedded seemingly forever to the politics of the territorial nation-state as its sole operating agency – the order recently seen and deployed as the principle of the planetary distribution of sovereignty and its imperturbable foundation – is now dying. Sovereignty is no longer glued to any of the elements of the territory/state/nation triad, let alone to a coordination and union between them; at the most, it is tied to them loosely and in parts, with those parts much reduced in size, content and importance. Sovereignty is nowhere complete; it is also, openly or surreptitiously, contested and eroded everywhere, facing ever new pretenders and competitors. The allegedly unbreakable marriage of power and politics (once firmly settled together in the government buildings of nation-states) is, on the other hand, coming to an end in separation, with the likely prospect of divorce.

Sovereignty nowadays is, so to speak, underdefined and contentious, porous and poorly defensible, unanchored and free-floating. The criteria for its allocation tend to be hotly contested, while the customary sequence of the principle of the allocation of sovereignty and its application is very often reversed (that is, that principle tends to be retrospectively articulated in the aftermath of an allocating decision, or deduced from an already accomplished state of affairs). Nation-states find themselves sharing the conflict-ridden, quarrelsome and aggressive company of actual, aspiring or pretending, but always pugnaciously competitive, quasi-sovereign subjects – entities successfully evading the application of the hitherto binding principle of *cuius regio, eius potestas, lex et religio* (he who rules holds the power, makes the law and chooses the religion), and all too often explicitly ignoring or stealthily sapping and impairing its intended objects. The ever-rising number of competitors for sovereignty have already outgrown, if not singly then surely in combinations of several, the holding and constraining power of an average nation-state (according to John Gray, multinational financial, industrial and trade companies now account 'for about a third of world output and two-thirds of world trade').[23] Sovereignty – that right to proclaim the laws as well as to suspend them and to make exceptions to their application at will, and the power to render these decisions binding and effective – is, for any given territory and any given aspect of life, fragmented, dissipated and scattered between a multiplicity of centres. For that reason, it is eminently questionable and open to contest. Multinationals can easily play one agency against another, thereby avoiding their involvement or interference, and escaping the supervision of any of them. No decision-making agency is able to plead full (that is unconstrained, indivisible, unshared) sovereignty, let alone claim it credibly and effectively.

The planet as a whole seems indeed to be in a state of interregnum these days. Extant political agencies bequeathed by the times before globalization are blatantly inadequate to cope with the new realities of planetary interdependency, while political tools potent enough to match the steadily rising capacities of powerful, though manifestly and self-admittedly non-political, forces are prominent mostly by their absence. Forces systematically escaping the control of established political institutions and recognizable as fully and truly global (such as capital and finances, commodity markets, information, criminal mafias, drug traffic, terrorism and the arms trade) are all of a kind: however much they may vary in other respects, they all stoutly, cunningly and astutely – encountering no effective (let alone intractable, impermeable or unpassable) obstacles – ignore or openly violate territorially enforced constraints, closely watched interstate borders and local (state-endorsed) statute books.

Where can new, universally (and that, for the first time in history, has to mean *globally*) respected and obeyed principles of human cohabitation come from, thereby marking the end of the 'interregnum'? Where can one look for likely agents to design them and put them into operation? In all probability, these quandaries constitute between them the greatest of the many challenges the current century will need to confront point-blank, dedicating most of its creative energy and pragmatic abilities to the search for an adequate response. Indeed, this is, one might say, a 'metachallenge', because, without confronting it, no other challenges, large or small, can conceivably be tackled. Whichever one of the countless dangers, risks and crises we consider, whether they are impending or already causing us trouble, the search for a solution invariably veers towards a truth we can ignore only at our – joint, shared, indivisible – peril: the truth that to global problems there can only be – if they exist at all – global solutions.

31

Whence the superhuman force – and what for?

Our perpetual state of uncertainty excretes a widespread and profound yearning for a *force* – any kind of force – that can be trusted to know for sure what the causes are of that deep yet vague and diffuse awareness or suspicion of insecurity that torments all too many ordinary people day and night in our liquid modern setting. The desire is that, knowing those causes, such a force might be able to instruct sufferers how to fight them effectively, disempowering and disabling them – or better still might be sufficiently potent itself to perform that task, where ordinary folk, cursed as they are with inadequacy of knowledge, skills and resources, can only dream of accomplishing it on their own. In short, there is a powerful yearning for a trustworthy and reliable force that can be counted on to see into the invisible and to confront point-blank what is evasive and treacherously hidden – one capable therefore of embracing the frighteningly unembraceable challenge and defeating an otherwise invincible adversary; and of doing all that promptly and thoroughly. To measure up to those expectations, the dreamed-of and sought-after force must be in a sense 'superhuman' – that is, free of familiar, common and frankly incurable human weaknesses, and resourceful enough to fight against, severely punish and stifle all resistance to its own resolutions and undertakings.

Such a force might be, as so often in past history, a 'living god'. In our times, it is more likely to be someone who, without pleading for divine status, claims to have received a revelation of the clandestine plotting and impending assault of evil forces beyond the reach and comprehension of lesser humans, and to have been anointed or predestined in another fashion for the mission of ruling and guiding the future victims on the road to salvation. It might be a single person claiming a personal right to be trusted by everyone on the grounds of something akin to a mission endorsed by heaven and a direct telephone line to the Almighty (like having access to classified security documents beyond the reach of others), and because of an exemplary and uniquely blameless character and inborn aversion to lying. Or it might be a collective body, like a church or a party, brandishing a blanket power of attorney signed, respectively, by God or History. Whatever the case, any variety of such a dreamed-of and superhumanly endowed force needs to claim its ability to salvage the perplexed from their perplexity and the impotent from their impotence: to annul the human weaknesses suffered singly or severally by the omnipotence of one chosen by God or History and the God-fearing or History-obeying congregation, nation, class or race.

God or History . . . two forces seen to be and assumed to be superhuman, matching a superhuman task. Whether they stay in alliance or happen to be at loggerheads, religious and political bodies aspire to control over the capitalization of the same resources (namely, human fears of ignorance and/or impotence). Like alternative brands on the market, they cooperate in beefing up demand for their products or vie with each other for the favours of the same prospective customers, claiming to satisfy the same need shared by their potential customers yet to offer more effective services than their competitors are deemed to be capable of mustering. Since openly brandishing the coercive nature of the intended subjugation (as practised by the rulers or conquerors of the past) is not a reasonable, and still less a plausible option, in the battle for the spirit waged amidst the multitude of freely mar-keted ideas, the reliance of the present-day *conquistadores* on the meekness, gullibility, diffidence or cowardice of the targeted 'cus-tomers' to be won and 'converted' to the brand is more often than not laboriously covered up.

In addition to the currently severely limited feasibility and rising pragmatic complexity of naked coercive power, resigning from its overt display and resorting instead to arguments and justifications has another reason to be seen as advantageous and to be preferred: the terrifying capacity of explicit threats tends to wear off relatively quickly. Populations cast in conditions of servitude and humiliating inferiority (whether by alien invaders, domestic authoritarian rulers or commercial interests) will sooner rather than later recover their guts and resolve to resist the usurpers, however overwhelming the latter's power and superiority might be, by voicing dissent and/or through a staunch refusal to cooperate. These populations will find ways to make the plight of their conquerors so uncomfortable that a prompt retreat would look incomparably more attractive than a continuation of their misery by clutching on to the invaded, yet obviously not really conquered, land. Conquerors and homebred tyrants alike prefer to present themselves as benefactors rather than confess their true intention, to claim to be bringing gifts (freedom, the prospect of affluence, the treasures of civilized life) rather than seeking the spoils of war and exacting tributes. All in all, religious and political bodies will most commonly aim at implanting and cultivating what Roberto Toscano and Ramin Jahanbegloo – taking inspiration from an essay written by Étienne de la Boétie half a millennium ago – suggest calling '*voluntary* servitude'.[24] La Boétie suspected that, in addition to the fear of punishment, the phenomenon of massive surrenders of substantive segments of their liberty by enslaved populations needed to be explained by an inner human compulsion to settle for order, *any order* (even an order severely short of freedom), rather than for a liberty that was bound to substitute contingency and uncertainty, those twin banes of the liquid modern world, among other forms of human cohabitation, for the kind of spiritual peace and comfort which only power-assisted routine (even an oppressive, constraining routine) can offer.

As bodies seeking political and religious power operate on the same territory, aim at the same clientele and promise to service similar needs, it is little wonder that they tend to exchange their techniques and strategies and to adopt, with only minor adjustments, each other's methods and arguments. Religious fundamentalisms borrow heavily from the inventory of socially produced troubles that are believed to be the domain and property of politics (perhaps even its defining property), whereas political (and ostensibly secular) fundamentalisms all too often deploy the traditionally religious language of the ultimate confrontation between good and evil, and practise the monotheistic inclination to sniff out, anathemize and exterminate every and any symptom, however minute, innocuous and marginal, of heresy or heterodoxy, or even of a mere indifference or lukewarmness attitude towards the (one and only) true doctrine. There is now a lot of talk about the 'politicization of religion'. Much too little attention is paid, however, to the parallel tendency, the so to speak 'religionization of politics', amply and unashamedly demonstrated by the last American administration, but all too common in the political vocabulary of our time in a more diluted while less explicit and sincere rendition. Conflicts of interests calling for negotiation and compromise (the daily bread of politics) are represented as ultimate showdowns between good and evil, a move that renders any negotiated agreement inconceivable. The two tendencies, I'd say, are truly inseparable Siamese twins, and in addition each is inclined to project what were once its own inner demons onto the other twin.

The late philosopher Leszek Kołakowski interpreted the phenomenon of religion as a manifestation and declaration of human insufficiency. Human togetherness creates problems it can't comprehend, or can't tackle, or both. Confronted with such problems, human logic risks floundering and foundering. Failing to twist the irrationalities it has spotted in the world to make them fit the tough frame of human reason, it cuts them off from the realm of human affairs and transports them into regions acknowledged to be inaccessible to human thought and action (incommensurability with human wits and capacities being the definition of God, and the concept of the Divine being composed of the qualities which humans yearn to possess while having no hope of ever acquiring them).

This is, by the way, why Kołakowski is on target when he points out that learned theologians have caused religion more harm than profit, and go on doing so, whenever they lean over backwards to supply 'logical proof' of God's existence. Humans have academic boffins and certified counsellors to serve and eulogize logic. They need God for his miracles, not for following the laws of logic; for his capacity of accomplish the abnormal, the out of the ordinary, the inconceivable, not for his ability to preserve and reinforce routine, the inevitable, the predetermined (it is for him to break out of or ignore these things, a feat which humans dream of but find it impossible to accomplish); for his inscrutability and incomprehensibility, not for transparency and predictability; for his ability to turn the course of events upside down; for his capacity to push aside the ostensibly intractable and indomitable order of things, instead of submitting to it slavishly, as humans are pressed to do and as most of them, most of the time, are resigned to doing. In short, human beings need an omniscient and omnipotent god (or his self-appointed earthly plenipotentiaries) to account for, and hopefully to tame and domesticate, all those awesome, apparently numb, dumb and blind forces which can't be reached by human comprehension and potency to act.

The futures of both contemporary pretenders to the status of superhuman forces – politics-like religion and the religion-like politics – are intertwined with the future of human uncertainty, of a condition continuously exacerbated by the realities of liquid modern life in both its renditions: of *collective* uncertainty (concerning the security and powers of the human species as a whole cast into, and dependent on, a natural world which it is unable to tame), and of *individual* uncertainty (concerning the security of the person, their social standing, their identity, when they find themselves cast into, and dependent on, a habitat which they, singly, severally or collectively, are unable to tame). Our abandonment and resulting loneliness in the universe, the absence of a court of appeal with executive powers that can be turned to in the event of a calamity too difficult for us to cope with, are too frightening for most human beings to bear. From this perspective, it looks as though God will die together with humanity – and not a moment earlier.

32

Back home, you men?

No one can know for sure how many redundancies will result from the present financial crisis. Everywhere in the world, the economy is in retreat; the statistics of economic activity and the production of wealth are falling fast or are about to fall, and the number of unemployed people relying on state benefits is growing with a speed the present generation has never experienced. The latest American statistics (see the *New York Times* of 7 November 2009) show that almost every fifth American has been seeking employment in vain or has abandoned the search after a year of trying unsuccessfully. (Unemployment figures are 17.5 per cent at present, but they keep rising – as assessed by David Leonhardt, 'they are the highest in decades', most probably higher than they were during the Great Depression of the 1930s: 'Nearly 16 million people are now unemployed and more than 7 million jobs have been lost since late 2007.') Rates of unemployment go on rising all over the planet . . .

There is little or rather very, very little that national governments can do to stem the tide, as the global dependencies and intertwining of national economies prevent them from reaching the faraway roots of the local troubles; the lightning speed with which the credit collapse affected even the most distant economies showed vividly just how dense our global interdependency had already become. Think: the sudden shortage of credit in the US caused many Americans to limit their consumption sharply (for a time at least); that in turn sharply cut American imports; China, a country with very rapidly developing industrial production and very rapidly growing exports of consumer products, thereby lost the largest of its markets; as a result, Chinese warehouses are bursting at the seams with unsold products, and numerous companies are going bankrupt or being forced to suspend production – and above all they are feeling obliged to shelve their projects for further expansion, no one can tell for how long; up to now, however, it was Chinese expansion that absorbed a greater part of the investment technology produced, first and foremost, in Japan and Germany; and so these two industrial giants also find themselves in trouble, as demand for their products and services shrinks.

All in all, the ranks of 'redundant people' are growing worldwide, a fact that in turn cuts worldwide consumption still further, which in turn pushes the number of unemployed up even faster – and so on and on . . . A vicious circle indeed; a self-propelling chain of causes and effects no one really knows how to interrupt or even slow down. The measures undertaken by governments around the world have brought mediocre results thus far, or have shown no effect at all as far as employment chances are concerned. One thing we can be certain of is that in the foreseeable future (once more, who knows for how long?) there will be fewer jobs on offer, and more people seeking them.

All those depressing observations are no longer news. But only now are we beginning to reflect on the likely consequences of the emerging and not yet fully explored economic conditions on such important aspects of our daily life as, for instance, the shape and the division of tasks inside the family. We can only guess that those consequences may be grave and far reaching – but how are they likely to change our relationships and the patterns of our daily interactions, as well as the ways we think about them and the forms we would wish them to take?

Take just one example. There are many signs (for as many reasons) that labour might be shed on the largest scale in the areas of economy (mainly 'heavy' industries) where the majority of employees have been traditionally, and until quite recently, male. The sectors known for their predominantly female labour force (like most services and shops) may be somewhat less affected by the depression. If this is indeed how things develop, the position of the husband and father as the principal breadwinner in the

family will receive another serious blow, and the habitual division
of labour and the entire pattern of life of the typical family could
be thrown back into the melting pot . . .

It is true that for many reasons, and as much by necessity as by
choice, working outside the home and holding a paid job has long
ceased to be an exclusively or even a predominantly male domain.
In a great number of families both husband and wife work outside
the family household. But in most cases the husband's income has
so far provided the larger share of the family budget – and despite
all the spectacular advances of women's liberation the condition
of staying at home and taking care of domestic chores while the
partner is out at work has been a less endearing prospect and a
less endurable plight for husbands than for their wives. And in the
event that the two career tracks collided and could not be easily
harmonized, priority was given more often than not (by mutual,
though not always whole-hearted and still more seldom joyful
consent) to the requirements of the husband's job. When new
family members were born, the 'natural' impulse was also, much
as before, for their mother to leave her job and dedicate her time
and energy to the children's care.

It may be (though we can't be sure) that this tacitly assumed
'logic of family life' will clash with the emergent 'logic of the
economy' and be exposed to powerful challenges as well as faced
with powerful pressures for it to be revised, renegotiated and
overhauled. The issues of women's equal rights to a professional
career, personal earnings, and more generally to access to the
public sphere and a weighty and consequential, if not fully equitable, presence therein, allegedly resolved once and for all, may
all be given another look and again become the objects of hot and
even acrimonious debate.

Even before the awareness and the realities of the economic
depression dawned on us, there were a few signs that this might
have already begun to happen. In the US, wide public debate is
heating up around Megan Basham's book *Beside Every Successful
Man: A Woman's Guide to Having It All*, in which the author
argues that helping the husband in promoting his career is more
profitable for both partners and for the family as a whole than
the situation in which both husband and wife pursue their careers
separately and they each put their share of money into the family
kitty. In purely financial terms, statistics seem to support Basham's

suggestion: men whose wives stay at home earn on average 31 per cent more than single men, but when both husband and wife hold full-time jobs, the advantage falls to a mere 3.4 per cent. To those average figures Basham adds the evidence of her own personal experience. She helped her husband, Brian, to establish himself in his position in television not only by 'being around' to offer moral support, or share in and soak up part of the tensions and frustrations generated by his career, but also virtually acted as her husband's copywriter and agent (unpaid, of course). She is proud of her contribution, and considers the impressive income brought home by Brian as their joint – a husband's *and* wife's – achievement: she was not a force 'behind' her husband, but as the title of her book suggests, stood and worked *beside* him (and she was not alone, she says: it was, after all, Michelle Obama who introduced Barack Obama to the political stage of Chicago).

That is, anyway, how Megan Basham feels. Not all her readers, though, find her feeling well justified. Crowds of often virulent critics have charged Basham with self-delusion and with a vicious attempt to mislead the sisterhood and arrest women halfway to genuine emancipation, or even to lure them into retreating from the far from finished war waged in its name. What Basham interprets as 'standing beside', her critics see as 'being cast into the shadow': as a case of discrimination, of denial of personal dignity – and an act of humiliation.

On one side, the critics. On the other, not entirely desired, perhaps even unexpected and unwelcome bedfellows. Shortly after Basham published her book, the American religious right made public its 'True Women Manifesto', pointing out that men and women have been created to reflect and to serve God in complementary and distinct ways, and that women belong in the home while men belong in the workforce; confusion of these places, the manifesto insists, leads to the destruction of the order of things as it was divinely ordained, an order not to be dabbled with and meant to remain forever intact.

The debate is far from over. On the contrary, it is gathering force. But now it is about to be joined by a participant thus far absent: unevenly rising unemployment after the economic depression. And the newly arrived discussant may claim, or gain without pleading, the decisive vote: the last word, at least in the current round of the argument. Be prepared.

33

Escape from crisis

Another reader of *La Repubblica*, David Bernardi, has asked what we can do to escape the alarming condition in which we've found ourselves following the collapse of credit, and how to avoid its possibly catastrophic consequences. He has asked, in other words, how each of us can and ought to behave and try to live – and what is the chance that other people will follow his or her good example.

These are questions which many of us ask ourselves today; after all, it is not only the banking system and stock exchange indices that have suffered severe blows – our confidence in the life strategies, ways of behaving, even the standards of success and the ideal of happiness which, as we were told day in, day out over recent years, were the ones worth pursuing, has also been shaken as they suddenly lost a considerable part of their authority and attraction. Our idols, the liquid modern versions of the biblical golden calves, melted away together with trust in our economy! As Mark Furlong of La Trobe University in Melbourne put it: 'All gone, down the gurgler . . . In full view, "the best and the brightest", the so-called "smartest guys in the room", got it spectacularly wrong.'[25]

In retrospect, those now bygone years before the credit crunch seem to have been times of a jaunty, easy-going, 'enjoy now, pay later' kind of life, navigated by a conviction that enough wealth would arise and expand tomorrow to quash any worries about the debts swelling today; so long as we did whatever was required to join those 'smartest guys in the room' and follow their example. In those now bygone years, climbing ever higher mountains and reaching ever more exhilarating vistas, dwarfing the towering mountains of yesterday into the hills of today and flattening the hills of yesterday into the gently undulating plains of today seem to have been destined to last forever. As one young and brilliant, incredibly successful, yet now bankrupt hedge fund dealer declared to millions of internauts: 'Nobody really ever lost – the ride had been running hard for so long. And then, whammo!'

Well, that orgy is now over. Days (months? years?) of reckoning have arrived. Days of hangover, and of sobering up. Perhaps also (hopefully) days of reflection, of thinking again about things that seemed to have been settled once and for all; of returning to the drawing board. Days also threatening or promising, portending or auguring (depending on our preferences!) the long days of Serge Latouche's *decroissance* (see his book *Farewell to Growth*).[26] His book describes the tightening of belts: returning to the years before the orgy, the years in which (as David Bernardi reminds us) there were fewer cosmetics and detergents, fewer automobiles on the roads, but also less rubbish and waste, fewer rejects and disparities, but plenty of energy and silence. Perhaps there will even be (as he suggests) years of less polluted air, with fewer buildings and more meadows ... Who knows? Who can be sure that this will happen? Is there a way back to the past (ways to be walked in real life, not just watched wistfully in Hollywood films)? Or is it rather, as Arabian folk wisdom insists, that men resemble their times more than they resemble their fathers?

Putting aside the notoriously risky game of prognostication or guessing, the practical point is how we can find our feet in whatever shape the landscape eventually assumes after the orgy. How will we be able to live, day in, day out, in a world half forgotten by the old and totally alien and unfamiliar to the young?

Some of the most acute analysts of the likely responses to that challenge, such as Lisa Appignanesi, predict a rapid rise in the frequency and spread of mental health problems. She argues that ' "depression" worldwide will soon be second in serious diseases only to heart disease and, in the developed world, will become the number one disease'. Depression? A reaction to the loss of illusions and the dissipation of sweet dreams, a feeling that the world around 'is going to the dogs' and we all, willy-nilly, are going with it – and that there is pretty little we can do to resist that descent or at least change its direction. Glenn Albrecht, of the University of Newcastle, investigated a while ago the psycho-social effects of the closing down of the mining industry on its insiders, the predominantly mining communities, and described 'the loss of wellbeing which follows the awareness that one's environment has suffered serious deterioration'.[27] The credit earthquake that shattered the financial towers left standing after the global terrorists' assault on the World Trade Center may have quite similar effects, and not only on its insiders.

There is another possible reaction to the present crisis, called by Mark Furlong the 'militarization of the self'. This is the kind of possibility which will tempt commercial interests that dearly wish to capitalize on the catastrophe by turning it into stockholder profit, as is their undying habit. The pharmaceutical industry is already in full swing, trying to invade, conquer and colonize that newly emerged 'virgin land' of post-crisis depression in order to sell its 'new generation' of 'smart drugs', starting with sowing, cultivating and making thrive the new illusions most likely to boost demand. We are already hearing of wondrous drugs that promise to make anyone who takes them regularly 'better than well', improving their memory, mood, sexual potency and energy levels and in this way offering total mastery over building themselves up, and making themselves prevail over the selves of others. Perhaps the world is indeed going to the dogs – let me, however, with the help of pharmaceutical inventions, become one of those dogs into whose laps it falls . . .

There is yet another possibility, though. There is the option of trying to get deeper down to the roots of the present trouble, and (as Furlong puts it), 'doing the opposite to that to which we have become accustomed: reversing the pattern organizing our thinking from one where "the individual" is placed at the centre to an alternative organized around an ethical and aesthetic practice privileging relationship and context'.

This is undoubtedly a long shot (some would even say a far-fetched or high-fallutin' prospect), calling for a protracted, tortuous and often painful period of self-criticism and readjustment. We were born and grew up in a thoroughly 'individualized' society, in which individual autonomy, self-reliance and self-centredness were all axioms needing no proof (nor indeed allowing any) – and permitting little, if any, discussion. Changes in one's worldview and a grasp of one's own place and role in society, as well as finding and choosing the proper way to proceed in it, do not come fast and easy. And yet this change seems to be imperative, indeed unavoidable.

Contrary to what is claimed of the spectacular 'emergency measures' lavished by governments on bank managers (though mostly with TV viewers in mind), there are no instant cures for prolonged, and possibly chronic, ailments. And there is little chance of curing the disease without willing and dedicated, and often arduous and self-immolating, cooperation from the patient. We are all patients where this particular socio-cultural disease is concerned, and so the cooperation of all and any of us is required. I believe that Serge Latouche's 'decrease', however firmly it stands to reason and however strongly advisable it may be, is far from being predetermined. It is just one of the alternative scenarios. Whether or not it is put on the stage of history depends on what we do, the actors in history and, in the last account, its unwitting playwrights.

34

Is there an end to depression?

Is the economic depression over? If not, how soon will it be? These and similar questions are asked daily by men and women, old and young, in rich and poor countries alike. They expect real answers in vain. To be sure, there is no shortage of answers, from economists (shouldn't they know if anyone does?), politicians in government and in opposition, and all sorts of other official or self-appointed soothsayers. The trouble is that they stretch all the way from joyous declarations of the end, or at least the last gasps, of the recession to dark warnings that the end of the tunnel is still nowhere to be seen . . .

In the *Guardian* of 9 September 2009 we find the information that 'economists have declared the recession over', illustrated by among others the opinion expressed by Karen Ward (UK economist at HSBC) that 'the things that were leading us into the downturn will lead us back out – we'll see positive consumer spending again'. Are we supposed to rejoice, or despair? Was it not 'positive consumer spending', and a lot of cash changing hands as a result (most of it not yet earned) that caused all that 'downturn' in the first place? Does not 'going back' presage similar, or still more horrifying, 'downturns' to come? And did not the collapse of the economy happen at the very peak of 'positive spending' and an unprecedented rise in GNP, universally (or almost universally) recognized as a measure of economic prosperity and an attribute of a 'healthy economy' as such? And, as Alex Berenson points out in an article under the telltale title, 'A Year after a Cataclysm, Little Change on Wall St' (*New York Times*, 12 September 2009), 'Wall Street lives on. One year after the collapse of Lehman Brothers, the surprise is not how much has changed in the financial industry, but how little' . . .

As long as the shock (called by some observers, with somewhat undue haste, a 'bitter awakening') stays fresh in the memory, we are painfully aware that the probability of predictions coming true is no greater than the likelihood of their rebuttal, and that the line separating trust from gullibility is thin, while there is no knowing in advance where that line should have been drawn in the first place.

No wonder we are cautious. We have every right to be. 'Consumers', the newspapers kept repeating until recently, and the *New York Times* perhaps most insistently among them, 'are reluctant to spend'. And this was widely taken as bad, frightening news – particularly for those of us who had the privilege of living in affluent countries, a privilege for which we have now been forced to pay. The higher you've climbed, the greater your fall will be. In the US, for instance, before the collapse of credit consumer spending constituted 70 per cent of total economic activity (that activity being measured, let's recall, by the amount of money changing hands); as 70 per cent of that money changing hands used to be pushed from the hands of consumers into the hands of the sellers of consumer goods, an even relatively minute and seemingly negligible fraction of consumers refusing to part with their cash (earned or that they hope to earn) is immediately reflected in the statistics on the 'state of the economy', causing another fit of panic that will surely make the prospect of recovering from the last fit still dimmer.

What the sellers of consumer goods bewail most is consumers losing their acquired habit of 'buying on impulse'. The theorists and practitioners of marketing used to count on that habit the most. One after another, shopping malls once proclaimed to be temples designed for congregations of thinking, knowing and potentially omniscient consumers were redesigned to tempt and seduce *accidental* buyers, 'buyers on impulse': people who went there to buy a replacement for a burnt pot or a light bulb, say, but – overwhelmed, inebriated and disarmed by the flood of colourful sights, ravishing sounds and intoxicating fragrances –

become prone to euphoria and ecstasy, and so likely to be suddenly stupefied and thrown into a trance by the sight of something
they have never seen before and never thought they needed, finding
themselves unable to resist the urge to possess it . . . But as Pat
Bennett, a salesman in Macy's chain of department stores, recently
complained (along with countless others charged with the seduction of consumers), that people nowadays tend to 'come in saying,
"I need a pair of underwear", and they get it and leave. You don't
really see them saying, "Oh, I love the way that shirt looks, and
I am just going to get it"' . . .

Replacing the old habit, deeply entrenched in their clients, of
buying in order to satisfy a need or to placate a long groomed and
carefully honed desire, with the habit of buying on impulse, on a
whim, on the spur of the moment was indeed the greatest feat of
the consumerist economy, and it fast turned into the flywheel of
its expansion. The disappearance of that habit would be nothing
short of an unmitigated disaster for that kind of an economy.
Buying in response to and motivated by need has its natural limits;
buying motivated by desire requires long, cumbersome and costly
cultivation, training and drilling of wishes; but buying on a whim
calls for no costly pump-priming and no lengthy and awkward
chores of honing and grooming, while the sky is its limit – and
the sky is the limit of a consumerist economy able to rely on that
propensity of its clients.

Or so it seemed at any rate: as long as we inhabited a make-
believe world of boundless and infinitely renewable consumer
credit, perpetually bloated stock-exchange indices, and an unstoppable and irreversible swelling in the value of homes. As long, that
is, as we felt richer than our current earnings could justify and
believed that this wondrous feeling would last forever. As long as
we could go on taking out mortgage loans on a future still undis-
closed, to be sure, but authoritatively promised (and strongly
believed) to hold 'more of the same bliss'. As long as we could keep
away the moment of reckoning, hold light-heartedly on to the
'enjoy now, pay later' life strategy with few if any afterthoughts,
and push back the moment of reckoning, of being called on or
forced to face up to, and compelled to seriously calculate, the risks
hidden in such a reckless strategy. Well, that 'pay later' day is now.

The arrival of that day must have come as a shock to all of us,
shocks tend to cause trauma, and traumas tend to last much longer

than their immediate causes. The depth and longevity of traumas are not the same for everybody affected, however. Most of us are reluctant nowadays to repeat yesterday's reckless behaviour – spending money we have not earned and becoming hostages to a fate we neither control nor are able to foresee; but as to the question of how long these unwelcome limitations imposed on our consumer feast (or orgy?) by an unfriendly fate will last, opinions differ.

In England, for instance, Londoners are three times more inclined than the residents of the industrial Midlands to believe that 'the economy is on the mend' and that over the next year it will improve. That gap is hardly surprising, considering that it took time for the recession to overflow from London's City banks to the factory floors of the Midlands, and that it will take a similar length of time, if not even longer, to chase it away from the households of jobless factory workers than from the homes of the beneficiaries of lavishly state-subsidized bank dividends and the profits of outfits servicing the rich. This is not a British peculiarity. The *New York Times* of 7 September 2009 reported on:

> millions of hidden casualties of the Great Recession who are not counted in the [official unemployment] rate because they have stopped looking for work. But that does not mean these discouraged Americans do not want to be employed. As interviews with several of them demonstrate, many desperately long for a job, but their inability to find one has made them perhaps the ultimate embodiment of pessimism . . .

There is another yawning gap between the sentiments of older and younger generations. Among people over 65, one in four trust the economy will improve in the coming year; among those who are 30 or more years younger, only one in twenty agree with their elders. Again, that is little wonder. People over 65 are almost all outside the labour market, whereas hapless insiders, full of dark premonitions, are still waiting for the blow to fall on their street, followed by a new string of bankruptcies, slimming exercises and massive redundancies. Those younger still face a future spattered with acts of humiliation and states of deprivation caused by social exclusion and the shame of joblessness, with the material hardship of long-term unemployment, long lines at job centres and employment agencies, and vain hopes of a speedy reversal of fortune and readmission to the ranks; given the latest frustration of expectations and dashing of hopes, who can swear that after any favourable turn (however unlikely in itself) the wheel of fortune would cease its wild gyrations? As late as 5 September 2009 the *New York Times* stated that 'the loss of 216,000 jobs in August, which pushed the jobless rate in the US to 9.7 percent, suggested that companies are not aggressively hiring despite signs of recovery.' The singed fingers of companies portend their employees' gutted livelihoods . . .

The youngest among the younger ones are, in addition, facing the hard realities of labour markets for the first time in their lives. Nothing in their relatively cloudless youth spent in a land of (fast or slow, but apparently infinitely) rising prosperity taught them to expect those markets to be as inhospitable and treacherous as they now discover them to be. Their friends just two or three years older remember that market as still being user-friendly, a labour market glutted with plum opportunities for them to pick and choose the juiciest; not a job market like the one they face – stingy with offers and lavish with rejections, able to dictate its terms of trade at will, niggardly with its graces and generous with its cruelties, notorious for its deadly equanimity towards human tragedies and the havoc its vagaries are bound to perpetrate in human lives.

This letter needs to be called a 'career report' – just like the assessments of our chances and handicaps that most of us are attempting to compose these days. The cards are still being shuffled; how strong or how weak the hands that are dealt will prove to be in the next game is anybody's guess. We are still in for many a surprise, many an unanticipated turn. If only we can carry from these experiences a lesson reaching further than the next shopping-mall escapade . . . a lesson reaching deeper – into the ways of forestalling this sort of experience from returning to haunt us and our children.

35

Who says you have to live by the rules?

This question is printed in large and bold letters at the top of the website www.locationindependent.com. And right beneath that question an answer is suggested:

> Are you fed up with having to live by the rules? The ones which say you have to work really hard, make lots of money just so you can buy a house with a big mortgage. And then work even harder to pay off that mortgage, until you can retire with a nice little nest egg pension . . . and finally start enjoying your life? That didn't sound great to us – and if it doesn't sound great to you, you've come to the right place.

Having read these words, I couldn't help recalling an old joke popular in the times of European colonialism: strolling in a leisurely way across the savannah, an Englishmen wrapped in the indispensable trappings of a proper colonialist's attire, topped with the obligatory tropical helmet, spots a native snoring sweetly in the shadow of a tree. The Englishman is overwhelmed with indignation, though it is tempered with his sense of the enlightening mission that brought him to the tropics. He kicks the sleeper out of his nap, shouting: 'Why are you wasting your time, you loafer, good-for-nothing lazybones?' 'What else could I do, Sir?' asks the newly woken native in reply, clearly bewildered. 'It is daytime, you should go to work!' 'What for?' the native asks, yet

more baffled. 'To earn money!' 'What for?' The native's amazement reaches its peak. 'To have some rest, to relax, to enjoy
leisure!' 'But this is precisely what I am doing!' It is now the
native's turn to sound offended and indignant.

Well, have we come full circle, are we now at the end of a long
detour, back to the starting point? Lea and Jonathan Woodward,
who run the 'location-independent' website, a highly educated and
skilled couple of European professionals – are they acknowledging, explicitly and directly rather than beating about the bush and
in a roundabout fashion, an inborn, intuitive premodern wisdom
that the pioneers, apostles and executioners of modernity decried,
ridiculed and tried hard to eradicate when they demanded instead
that people should work hard throughout their lives only in order
finally, at the far end of interminable drudgery, to 'start enjoying
it'?! To them, just as it was to the 'native' in the anecdote, the
silliness of such a proposal is so dazzlingly obvious that it needs
neither elaboration nor discursive proof. To them, as it was to
that 'native', it is crystal clear that putting work before leisure,
and so obliquely delaying potentially instantaneous satisfaction
– that sacrosanct rule piously obeyed by the colonialist in the
anecdote and his contemporaries – is no wiser, and no more
useful, than putting a cart before a horse.

For the Woodwards to acquire such self-assurance, to pro-
nounce with such confidence views still classified as an abominable
heresy a generation or two earlier, a major 'cultural revolution'
was needed; not just in the worldview of the knowledge classes,
but in the world they were born into, grew up in, came to know
and lived through. To sound obvious, their life philosophy had to
be grounded in current realities and firm material foundations
which no powers-that-be seem to be set on undermining.

The foundations of the old/new life philosophy seem by now
to be indeed unshakeable. Just how profoundly and irreversibly
the world was changed on the way to the 'liquid' phase of modernity has been manifested by the timidity of governmental reactions
to the greatest economic catastrophe since the end of the 'solid'
phase: ministers and lawmakers set out, well-nigh instinctively, to
save the financial industry, together with the pursuit of perks,
bonuses, stock exchange 'killings' and platinum handshakes that
kept it on its course: that powerful causal and operational force
behind deregulation, and the major promoter and practitioner of

the philosophy of 'we will start worrying about crossing that bridge when we come to it', of actions sliced into episodes sanitized against responsibility for the consequences, of a life on credit and on borrowed time, of a life pattern of 'enjoy now, pay later'. In other words, the selfsame power-assisted habits to which the causes of the economic earthquake in question could (and should) be ultimately traced.

Instead of trying to reach and stem the sources of the trouble, governmental intervention vociferously endorsed the culprits, publicly and demonstratively countersigning their legitimacy and indispensability and decreeing their preservation and reinforcement to be in the 'national interest'. As *New York Times* correspondents informed us on 13 September 2009, 'if you take out a car loan or run up your credit card, the chances are good that the government is financing both your debt and that of your bank.' But 'far from eagerly micromanaging the companies the government owns, Mr Obama and his economic team have often laboured mightily to avoid exercising control even when government money was the only thing keeping some companies afloat'. The governments attempted to remove the odium from the 'heads I win, tails you lose' tactics of the moneylenders – by converting the stigma of unconcern and dangerously carefree attitudes into badges of prudence and good understanding of the national interest, if not of supreme patriotism. And it achieved this effect by brandishing a governmental addition and complement to the quoted precept of the moneylenders' tactics: 'heads you win, tails you're bailed out.'

In the Woodwards' appeal more is at stake, much more, than the issue of whether a workplace is fixed to the ground or mobile, enclosed inside a single office block or travelling through a favoured selection of countries, including Thailand, South Africa and the Caribbean; and it is more than being 'fed up with the instability of the rat race and working for other people' (the experience that, as they suggest, prompted them to invent the idea, develop the lifestyle and build 'the mindset of independence from location'). What is truly at stake is, as they admit, the 'freedom to choose what's right for you'. For *you* – not 'for *other* people', or for that matter how the place and the earth should be shared with those others. But by making that principle into a yardstick by which the propriety and worthiness of life attitudes are measured, the

Woodwards (a charge they would most probably indignantly reject) see eye-to-eye with the people they rebel against, bosses like the board of directors and managers of Lehman Brothers and their innumerable imitators; with the countless practitioners of, as Alex Berenson of the *New York Times* put it, 'eight-figure paydays'.

They are all, unanimously, in favour of the 'order of egoism' taking precedence over that 'order of solidarity' whose most fertile greenhouse and principal citadel used to be the protracted (deemed infinite) sharing of offices and factory floors. It was the boards of directors and managers of multinational corporations, with overt or tacit support and encouragement from the political powers of the day, who undertook to explode the foundations of employees' solidarity through the abolition of collective bargaining, the disarming of associations of employee self-defence, forcing them off the battlefield, manipulation of the terms of employment, 'outsourcing' and 'contracting out' managerial functions and employees' responsibilities, deregulating ('flexibilizing') working hours, shortening labour contracts while simultaneously intensifying staff rotation, and making the renewal of contracts dependent on closely and continuously monitored individual performance; that is, to put it in a nutshell, doing everything possible to undercut the rationality of collective self-defence and increase the attraction of cut-throat individual competition for managerial favours.

The ultimate step on the road to putting paid once and for all to any chance of employee solidarity – for the great majority of people the sole reliable vehicle of the 'freedom to choose what is right for you' – would require, however, the abolition of the 'fixed workplace', the shared office or factory floor. That was the step that was taken by Lea and Jonathan Woodward. With their types of skills and credentials they could afford to take it. Not many, however, will be in a position to seek a remedy for their unfreedom in Thailand, South Africa or the Caribbean, in that or any other order. For those many who are not in such a position, the Woodwards' new concept/lifestyle/mindset would clinch the finality of their losses, as fewer people would remain to join forces in the collective defence of their individual freedoms, and as those who would be ever more conspicuous by their absence would be the 'knowledge classes', who once had the mission of lifting the downtrodden and the left-behind out of their misery.

But what about Woodwards' gain? That remains to be seen: can one indeed find effective individual solutions to socially produced problems? There is some last-moment news added to the 'location-independent' website: 'Lea & Jonathan have just had a baby girl (unplanned & very unexpected!) – born, quite appropriately, on the 4th of July. They are planning to resume their travels at the end of 2009, with the babe in tow.' We should wish them all the luck in facing up to their new realities. There will be more new realities (as they say, 'unplanned & very unexpected'!) that they will have to face in the years to come. And by then they will only have each other to help in confronting those realities and tackling their challenges.

36

The phenomenon of Barack Obama

In an interview conducted a few months before the last American presidential elections, Giuliano Battiston asked me the following question:

> During the electoral campaign Barack Obama has never claimed an exclusivist ethnic identity (rather, he called himself a 'mixed' person), and has never tried to play the politics of identity card, adopting the so-called culturalist version of identity, to such an extent that some observers define him as the first 'post-essentialist' American president. Could his election be interpreted as a sign that the American political system has definitively broken the link between *demos* and *ethnos* and that America is going toward a more conscious post-ethnic society?

To which I then answered:

'Let me rephrase the problem . . . Obama was careful to bid for power *not* in the name of the 'downtrodden and oppressed' masses, who are for that reason proclaimed inferior – and whose imposed and stereotyped ineptitude, indignity and infamy rubbed off on him because of his ethnically/racially inherited assignment. And he did not come to power on a wave of rebellion by the 'downtrodden and oppressed' or by a 'social/political movement', as their spokesman, plenipotentiary and avenger. What his advance and elevation was intended to prove – as in all probability it did

– was that a collective stigma can be washed away from selected individuals; in other words, that some *individuals* among categories oppressed and discriminated against possess qualities that 'outweigh' their participation in a collective, *categorial* inferiority; and the qualities may equal, or even surpass those boasted of by competitors unburdened by the categorial stigma. Such a phenomenon does not necessarily invalidate the assumption of categorial inferiority. It may be perceived (and is by many) as a perverse reassertion of the assumption: here is an individual who, almost in Baron Münchhausen's style, has lifted himself by his own bootstraps out of the bog, through his individual talents and stamina, not *thanks* to his belonging but *despite* it, and proving by the same token not so much the grossly underestimated virtues of 'his people' as the tolerance and generosity of those ready to make exceptions by closing their eyes to collectively carried defects – providing the individual in question fights gallantly and successfully to erase them. This is, indeed, a roundabout restatement of the infallibility of the underlying assumption and propriety of the order of things to which it refers: that *some* individuals make it because of earnestly trying shows and proves that the rest, the massive majority that 'failed to make it', are to drown in their misery because of their sloth and/or inherent ineptitude. (Apparently astonishing news is flowing in – though in the light of such considerations not at all astonishing – that the American 'far right' is rejoicing in, and celebrating the elevation of Obama.)

'Of course, the feat accomplished by Obama will embolden more ambitious and talented individuals from the category discriminated against to try to follow suit; and quash many an objection as well as soften resistance to the social and political acceptance of those who succeed. This does not mean, though, that their advance will lift the 'category as such' from its inferior social position and open wider life prospects to all its members. The long semi-dictatorial rule of Margaret Thatcher did not bring the social equality of women. What it proved was that *some* women may defeat men at their own macho game. Many of the Jews who managed to emerge from the ghettos in the nineteenth century and pass for Germans (or so they tried to believe) did pretty little for the ascribed or imputed brethren they left behind to lift them out of poverty and protect them from legal and social discrimination. Many of the most vociferous and dedicated ideologues and practitioners of the most radical varieties of the nationalisms up and coming in the twentieth century were newcomers from 'ethnic minorities', or 'naturalized' foreigners (Stalin and Hitler included). A Jewish Benjamin Disraeli solidified and fortified the Empire of the British. The warcry of all the 'assimilated' was 'anything you can do, I can do better' – a promise and determination to be more catholic than the Pope, to out-German the Germans, out-Pole the Poles, out-Russian the Russians in enriching *their* culture and promoting *their* 'national interests' (which, by the way, in numerous cases was held against them and taken as a proof of their duplicity and insidious intentions). In all such cases, it was the inhabitants of the destination world who were accorded the undisputed right to judge the success or failure of the efforts at assimilation, according to criteria they set themselves. Among all those things they were bent on 'doing better' than the natives were also, for many of the assimilated, the contempt and reproof felt and expressed by the 'natives' for the genuine or putative ways and means of the 'community of origin' of the assimilated.

'Obviously, reasoning by analogy, as with knowledge of statistical trends, makes one think, but it does not enable one to predict what will happen in any particular case. However massive a majority might be that allows one to speak of a "trend" or a "rule", there is always ample room for exceptions. Please interpret my answer to your question as a call to be cautious in prognosticating and to abstain from jumping to conclusions.'

A little more than a year later, one can confront those 'cautious prognostications' and warnings against premature conclusions with the story of the first chapter of Obama's presidency. Naomi Klein summed up the experience of the latter:

> Non-elite blacks and Latinos are losing significant ground, with their homes and jobs slipping away from them at much higher rate than from whites. So far, Obama has been unwilling to adopt policies specifically geared toward closing this ever-widening divide. The result may well leave minorities with the worst of all worlds: the pain of a full-scale racist backlash without the benefits of policies that alleviate daily hardships.[28]

37

Culture in a globalized city

Cities, and particularly megacities like London, are the dustbins into which problems produced by globalization are dumped. They are also laboratories in which the art of living with those problems (though not the art of resolving them) is experimented with, put to the test and (hopefully, hopefully . . .) developed. The most seminal impacts of globalization (above all, the divorce of power from politics, and the shifting of functions once undertaken by political authorities sideways, to the markets, and downwards, to the realm of individual life-politics) have been thoroughly investigated by now and described in great detail. In this letter, I will therefore confine myself to one aspect of the globalization process, too seldom considered in connection with the paradigmatic change in the study and theory of culture: namely, the changing patterns of global migration.

There were three different phases in the history of migration in the modern era.

The first wave of migration followed the logic of a tripartite syndrome: *territoriality* of sovereignty, '*rooted*' identity, a *gardening* posture (these are subsequently referred to, for the sake of brevity, as TRG). That was emigration from a 'modernized' centre (read: a site of intense order-building and economic progress, the two main industries that turned out, and off, growing numbers of 'wasted humans'), partly an exportation and partly an eviction of up to 60 million people (a huge amount by the nineteenth-century standards) to 'empty lands' (read: lands whose native populations could be struck out of the 'modernized' calculations; be literally uncounted and unaccounted for, presumed either non-existent or irrelevant, nothing to reckon with). Any native residents still alive after massive slaughters and mass epidemics were proclaimed by the settlers, and those who sent them and went on multiplying their numbers, to be objects of the 'white man's civilizing mission'.

The second wave of migration could best be described as a case of the 'Empire emigrates back'. With the dismantling of colonial empires, a number of indigenous people in various stages of 'cultural advancement' followed their colonial superiors to the metropolis. On arrival, they were cast in the metropolis according to the only worldview and strategic mould available to it from its past experience: one designed, formed and used in the nation-building era to deal with minorities earmarked for 'assimilation' in the emergent national community. It was a power-assisted process aimed at suppressing and annihilating their cultural dissimilarity, putting the 'minorities' at the receiving end of crusades, *Kulturkampf* and proselytizing missions (currently renamed, in the name of 'political correctness', 'citizenship education aimed at integration'). This story is not yet finished: like Minerva's Owl, known to spread its wings at the end of the day, its echoes reverberate time and again in the declarations of intent voiced by politicians in public view. As in the first phase of migration, the drama of the 'empire migrating back' attempted to operate inside the frame of the now outdated TRG syndrome, yet with little if any success.

The third wave of modern migration, now in full force and still gathering momentum, led into the age of *diasporas*: archipelagos of ethnic, religious and linguistic settlements criss-crossing the world – oblivious to the trails blazed and paved by the imperialist-colonialist episode and following instead a globalization-induced logic of the planetary redistribution of life resources. Each diasporic archipelago tends to be diffuse and widely scattered. Each stretches over many separate and nominally sovereign territories, ignoring the territorial claims of local demands and obligations to superiority and supremacy, and as a result tending to be locked into the double (or multiple) bind of 'dual (or multiple) nationality' and dual (or multiple) loyalty. Present-day migration differs from the two previous phases in one more respect: it moves both ways (nowadays virtually all countries, including Britain, are lands of immigration and emigration simultaneously), without privileged routes (routes are no longer determined by the imperial/ colonial links of the past). It also differs in exploding the old TRG syndrome and replacing it with an EAH one (*extraterritoriality*, '*anchors*' displacing 'roots' as primary tools of identification, a *hunting* strategy).

The new migration casts a huge question mark over the bond between identity and citizenship, individual and place, neighbourhood (or physical proximity) and belonging. Jonathan Rutherford, an acute and insightful observer of the fast-changing frames of human togetherness, notes that the residents of the London street where he lives form a neighbourhood of different communities, some with networks extending only to the next street and others with networks that stretch across the world.[29] It is a neighbourhood of porous boundaries in which it is difficult to identify who belongs and who is an outsider. What is it we belong to in this locality? What is it that each of us calls home and, when we think back and remember how we arrived here, what stories do we share?

Living (as so many do) *in* a diaspora (how far does it stretch, and in which direction(s)?), and like all of us *among* diasporas (how far do they stretch and in which direction(s)?) has for the first time forced on to the agenda the issue of the 'art of living with difference' – a problem and a task that may appear on the agenda only once the difference and dissimilarity are no longer seen as merely temporary irritants, and so, unlike in the past, urgently require the development of new arts and skills, teaching them and learning them. The idea of 'human rights', promoted in the setting of EAH to replace or complement the TRG institution of territorially determined identity, today translates as the 'right to remain different'. By fits and starts, that new rendition of the human rights idea lays down the sediment of, at best, *tolerance*; it has as yet to start in earnest to lay down the sediment of *solidarity*. And it is a moot question whether it is capable of conceiving group solidarity in any other form than that of fickle and frayed, predominantly virtual 'networks', galvanized and continually remodelled by the interplay of individuals connecting and disconnecting, making calls and declining to reply to them.

The new rendition of the human rights idea disassembles hierarchies and tears apart the imagery of upward ('progressive') 'cultural evolution'. Forms of life float, meet, clash, crash, catch hold of each other, merge or separate and hive off with (to deploy Georg Simmel's metaphor) equal specific gravity. Steady and stolid hierarchies and evolutionary lines are replaced with battlefields of claims and counterclaims, pleas for and resistance against recognition – with the battles leading at best to yet another pecking order, frail, fissiparous and eminently renegotiable in just the same way as the orders it came (temporarily) to replace. Imitating Archimedes, who was reputed to insist (probably with the kind of desperation only the utter nebulousness of the project might have caused) that he could turn the world upside down provided he was given a solid enough fulcrum, we might say that we could tell who should assimilate to whom, whose dissimilarity or idiosyncrasy should be destined for the chop and whose should emerge on top, provided we were given a hierarchy of cultures. Well, we are not given one, and are unlikely to be given one soon.

38

The voice of Lorna's silence

In one of the first scenes of the film by Jean-Pierre and Luc Dardennes, *Le silence de Lorna*, the eponymous heroine, exquisitely played by Artya Dobroshi, opens her mailbox, only to be frustrated; once again she finds it empty of the long-awaited letter. As the plot unravelled, it dawned on me that what I was watching, with bated breath, was itself a letter: a letter from the liquid modern world and one I would dearly have wished to write myself but would have failed, lacking the cinematographic vision and story-telling talents of the two directors and the writers of the screenplay. That wish of mine being, alas, bound to stay forever unfulfilled, the only thing I can do is to explain why I believe the oeuvre of Jean-Pierre and Luc Dardennes to be one of the best letters from the liquid modern world ever written . . . At least one of the best I've had a chance to read or managed to imagine.

The film does not start immediately with the search for the letter: it starts (and ends as well) like most plays staged in our liquid modern times (tragedies and comedies alike): with a sum of money changing hands. The film starts with Lorna, an immigrant with a temporary residence permit but applying for Belgian citizenship, paying some money into her bank account. The film ends with Lorna emptying and closing her account and being stripped of her Belgian identity card and mobile telephone (read: her network of connections, of people she might call, her sole anchorage amidst raving tides), and facing a choice between physical death and social death. The final credits splash on to the screen a few moments later, with Lorna, having been abandoned by friends and having escaped her persecutors, lying down for the night, stripped of all her tokens of identity or belonging, on a table in an abandoned wooden shack, deep in the woods in the middle of nowhere.

Lorna was married to Claudy, a junkie, who agreed to offer himself to Lorna as a path to Belgian citizenship – in exchange for a round sum of euros to finance his drug addiction. We learn that Fabio, the head of a mafia-like trade in passports, hearing the purpose of the frankly fictitious marriage, saw Claudy's drug addiction as a major virtue: junkies die fast, he stated, and if they don't die fast enough, then an overdose (whether by their own mistake or helped by others' cleverness and malice aforethought) as a way of speeding up their departure was always a credible, since highly probable, eventuality. Then the young widow, having become a fully fledged Belgian citizen, would be able to offer her hand in marriage to another citizenship-seeker, for another round sum of euros . . . Lorna and her lover, Sokol (also an immigrant of, so to speak, eminently 'fluid' status), plan to use the money, eventually topped up with a hefty bank loan, to open a snack bar and start selling sandwiches for a change instead of their own bodies and identities.

In a society of consumers – that is, of people who, in order to consume, first need to offer themselves on the consumer market as sellable commodities – all that must have seemed a flawlessly calculated business proposition. It was perfectly attuned to the logic and spirit of the society which Lorna and Sokol were struggling to enter, much like the prospective buyers of their services, including their legally defined identities – the society in which they dreamed of becoming settled and secure. The scheme soon started falling apart, though, ripped asunder by factors the business proposition had neglected for the simple reason that they lacked a market price: factors such as compassion, pity, an impulse to care, or distaste for the infliction of pain and aversion to the sight of human suffering did not figure in the 'marital' contract.

These factors could be left out of the contract but, as became clearer by the day, they could not be kept out of human cohabitation and interaction for long. Faced with Lorna, a decent, hard-working, honest person, Claudy is inspired to lift himself out of his human degradation, by his bootstraps if necessary – and quit the destructive habit. Claudy's appeals for help, and still more the sorry sight of Claudy struggling to defeat his degrading affliction yet tormented by cruel withdrawal symptoms, interfere brutally, and in the end successfully, with both the large and the small print of the business proposition. Lorna is human, Lorna cares, Lorna is urged to help – by what? Not by her contractual obligations, for sure. Perhaps, then, by her humanity? By the distress and agony she sees on the face of another human being?

When the long-awaited letter with the decree nisi finally arrives and Claudy faces the prospect of losing Lorna, Claudy again turns to the drug pusher for the sole medicine against despair he knows and has tested . . . Lorna kicks the pusher out, however, locks the door and throws the key out of the window to make sure that the morbid temptation won't return. She then undresses and offers her body to Claudy as an alternative medicine. The medicine seems to be working . . .

But so are the divorce procedures. What we learn next is that Claudy dies of an overdose. Suicide? A mistake? Murder? We are not told; and neither can Lorna be sure. *She* might have been left in the dark, but her conscience was not, and could not be double-crossed. Lorna used to treat Claudy as a commodity, so her conscience whispers; she bought him as a potentially, profitable commodity, an investment stock, a step on the ladder she hoped to use to lift herself into a higher price category. But it is too late now to compensate Claudy for the pain he suffered as a result, to repent and make amends for the harm she has done . . .

Too late, indeed? Not for those ready and willing to pay the price of regaining a clear conscience. The costs are huge – few would agree to pay them. Lorna accepts the price – she opts out of the market. She declares that she has been made pregnant by Claudy, and refuses the abortion which both Fabio and Sokol unconditionally demand; pregnant, Lorna loses her value on the immigration market and her prospective 'husband' demands his money back. Her downpayment on the dreamed-of snack bar is lost. Fabio writes Lorna off on the debit side and earmarks her for speedy and discreet disposal. Sokol, while deeply disappointed and robbed of his dreams, washes his hands of the whole affair and heads for greener (or, rather, not yet scorched) pastures. Lorna is no longer a player. She is not even a stake in other people's games, no longer a prospective hunting trophy. Purely and simply, she is useless. Another item on the long list of wasted humans.

Lorna runs away from it all to the abandoned shack, a piece of waste like herself, abandoned like herself in a desolate, featureless nowhere-land reminiscent of those other-worldly, Elysian fields – leaving behind all her belongings (read: all traces and deposits of her past life). She will now dedicate her remaining life to the care and protection of an-other: the imagined child of Claudy whom, in the absence of other humans, she has convinced herself she is carrying in her womb – contrary to learned medical opinion, seasoned as it is in spotting and treating bodily ailments, but considerably less apt at doing the same with diseases of the spirit . . .

I've related the film of the Dardennes as a powerful dramatic metaphor for the choices we face and the prices that need to be paid for choices we make. I wonder whether you agree with me, and if you do, whether you've arrived at that agreement following a similar route to mine . . .

39

Strangers are dangers . . . Are they, indeed?

Whatever happens to cities in their history, one feature remains constant: cities are spaces where strangers stay and move in close proximity to each other. The ubiquitous presence of strangers, constantly within sight and reach, inserts a large dose of perpetual uncertainty into the life pursuits of all city dwellers; that presence is a prolific source of anxiety, never resting, and of a usually dormant aggressiveness that nevertheless erupts time and again.

Strangers also provide a convenient – handy – outlet for our inborn fears of the unknown, uncertain and unpredictable. In chasing strangers away from our homes and streets, we exorcise the frightening ghost of insecurity born of uncertainty, if only for a moment: the horrifying yet irritatingly elusive monster is burnt, at least in effigy. These exorcisms do not leave our liquid modern life unscathed, however, and certainly not reformed: it goes on exuding insecurity, remaining stubbornly uncertain, erratic and capricious. Any relief is bound to be short-lived, and even the hopes attached to the toughest of measures taken against the putative carriers of uncertainty will be dashed as soon as they are raised . . .

This consideration, though, isn't much help to the stranger's lot. The stranger is, by definition, an agent moved by intentions which can be guessed at best – but of which we can never be sure. In all the equations we compose when we are deliberating about what to do and how to proceed with what we have decided, the stranger is an unknown variable. A stranger is, after all, 'strange': a bizarre being whose intentions and reactions may be thoroughly different from those of ordinary (common, familiar) folks. And so, even when they are not behaving aggressively or explicitly resented, strangers are discomforting: their sheer presence makes the already daunting task of predicting the effects of our actions and our chances of success into a still taller order. And yet sharing space with strangers, living in their proximity (as a rule uninvited and unwelcome), is a condition that city residents find it difficult, and probably impossible, to escape.

As the proximity of strangers is the urban dweller's non-negotiable fate, a modus vivendi to make cohabitation palatable and life liveable *must* be designed, tried and tested. The way we go about gratifying this need is a matter of *choice*, however. And we make choices daily, whether by commission or omission, by design or default; by conscious decision or just by blindly and mechanically continuing in customary ways; by wide-ranging discussion and deliberation, or just by following trusted, because currently fashionable, patterns. Opting out altogether from the search for a better mode of cohabitation with the strange and the strangers is one of the possible choices. 'Mixophobia' is a foremost example of that choice.

Mixophobia manifests itself in a drive towards building islands of similarity and sameness amidst the sea of variety and difference. The reasons for mixophobia are banal – easy to understand, though not necessarily easy to forgive. As Richard Sennett has suggested, 'the "we" feeling, which expresses a desire to be similar, is a way for men to avoid the necessity of looking deeper into each other.' It promises thereby some spiritual comfort: the prospect of making togetherness easier by making redundant any effort to understand, negotiate and compromise. 'Innate to the process of forming a coherent image of community is the desire to avoid actual participation. Feeling common bonds without common experience occurs in the first place because men are afraid of participation, afraid of the dangers and the challenges of it, afraid of its pain.'[30] The drive towards a 'community of similarity' is a sign of withdrawal not just from the otherness outside, but also from commitment to the lively yet turbulent, engaged yet no doubt cumbersome interaction inside.

Choosing the escape option guided by mixophobia has an insidious and deleterious consequence of its own: the more self-perpetuating and self-reinforcing that strategy is, the less effective it is. The longer the time people spend in the company of others 'like them', 'socializing' perfunctorily and matter-of-factly with them to avoid the risk of miscomprehension and the still more onerous and off-putting need to translate between distinct universes of meaning, the more they are likely to 'de-learn' the art of negotiating shared meanings and a mutually gratifying mode of cohabitation. As they've forgotten the skills needed to live with difference, or neglected to acquire them in the first place, they view the prospect of confronting strangers face-to-face with rising apprehension. Strangers tend to appear ever more frightening as they become increasingly alien, unfamiliar and incomprehensible, and as the mutual communication which could eventually accommodate and assimilate their 'otherness' to one's own lifeworld fades, or fails to take off. The drive to a homogeneous, territorially isolated environment may be triggered by mixophobia, and the practising of territorial separation is that mixophobia's lifebelt and source of nourishment.

It all started in the US, but leaked into Europe and has by now spilt into most European countries: the tendency for better-off urban dwellers to buy themselves out of the crowded city streets where anything can happen and little can be predicted, and into 'gated communities', walled-off developments with strictly selective entry, surrounded by armed guards and stuffed with closed-circuit TV and anti-intruder alarms. Those lucky few who have bought themselves into a closely guarded 'gated community' pay an arm and a leg for 'security services': that is, for the banishment of all mixing. Gated 'communities' are little heaps of private cocoons suspended in a spatial void.

Inside 'gated communities' the streets are mostly empty. And so if someone who 'does not belong', a *stranger*, appears on the sidewalk, he or she will be promptly spotted as an out-of-the-ordinary event – before a prank or damage can be done. As a matter of fact, anybody you see walking past your window or front door can fall into the category of strangers, those frightening people who make you feel you can't be sure of their intentions or of what they will do next. Anyone may be, unknown to you, a prowler or a stalker: an intruder with ill intentions. We live, after all, in the time of mobile phones (not to mention MySpace, Facebook and Twitter): friends can exchange messages instead of visiting, all or almost all the people we know are or can be constantly 'online' and able to inform us in advance if they are planning to pop in – and so a sudden, unannounced knock at the door or ringing of the bell is an extraordinary event and a signal of potential danger. Inside a 'gated community', the streets are kept empty – to render the entry of a stranger, or someone behaving like a stranger, too risky to be tried.

The side-effect or corollary of emptying the streets is that the term 'gated *community*' becomes, for all practical intents and purposes, a misnomer. As we read in a 2003 research report published by the University of Glasgow, there is 'no apparent desire to come into contact with the "community" in the gated and walled area . . . Sense of community is lower in gated "communities".' However the inhabitants (and their estate agents) may justify their choices, they do not pay exorbitant rental or purchase prices in order to find themselves in, or found, a 'community' – that notoriously intrusive and obtrusive 'collective busybody', opening its arms to you only to hold you down as if by steely forceps. Even if they say (and sometimes believe) otherwise, people pay all that money in order to *liberate* themselves from any company except that of their choice and at the time of their choice. They pay, ultimately, for the privilege of *being left alone*. Inside the walls and the gates live loners: people who will only tolerate as much 'community' as they fancy at that moment, and for no longer than that moment of fancying it . . .

A large majority of researchers agree that people's main motive in locking themselves inside the walls and the CCTV of a 'gated community' is, consciously or subconsciously, explicitly or tacitly, their desire to keep the wolf from the door, which they translate as keeping strangers at arm's length. Strangers are dangers, and so every stranger is a container and a portent of danger. Or so at least they believe. And what they wish more than anything else is to be secure from danger. More exactly, though, to be secure from the daunting, harrowing, incapacitating *fear of insecurity*. They hope that the walls will protect them from that fear.

The snag is, however, that there is more than one reason to feel insecure. Whether credible or fanciful, the rumours of rising crime and throngs of burglars or sexual predators lying in ambush and waiting for an occasion to strike are just one of those reasons. After all, we feel insecure because our jobs, and so our incomes, social standing and dignity, are under threat. We are not insured against the threat of being made redundant, excluded and evicted, losing the position we cherish and believe we have earned the right to forever. Nor are the partnerships we cherish foolproof and secure: we may feel subterranean tremors and expect earthquakes. Our familiar cosy neighbourhood may be threatened with being run down in order to clear the site for a new development. All in all, it would be downright silly to hope that all these well-founded or ill-founded anxieties can be placated and put to rest by surrounding ourselves with walls, armed guards and TV cameras.

But what about that (ostensibly) prime reason to opt for a 'gated community' – our fear of physical assault, violence, burglary, car theft, obtrusive beggars? Won't we at least put paid to *that* kind of fear? Alas, even on that front the gains hardly justify the losses. As signalled by the most acute observers of contemporary urban life, the likelihood of being assaulted or robbed may diminish once someone has retreated behind walls (though research into 'feelings of safety' conducted recently in California, perhaps the main stronghold of the obsession with 'gated communities', found no difference between gated and non-gated spaces), but the persistence of fear will not. Anna Minton, the author of a thorough study of *Ground Control: Fear and Happiness in the Twenty-First Century City*,[31] relates the case of Monica, who 'spent the whole night lying awake and far more scared than she had ever been in the twenty years she had lived on an ordinary street' when 'one night the electronically controlled gates went wrong and had to be propped open'. Behind the walls, anxiety *grows* instead of dissipating – and so does the dependence of the residents' state of mind on 'new and improved' high-tech gadgets, marketed with the promise to put dangers, and the fear of dangers, out of court. The more gadgets one has surrounded oneself with, the greater the fear that some of them may 'get it wrong'. The more time is spent worrying about the menace carried by every stranger, the less time is spent in the company of strangers so that the worry can be put to the test. The further that 'tolerance and appreciation for the unexpected recedes', the less possible it is to confront, handle, enjoy and appreciate the liveliness, variety and vigour of urban life. Locking oneself inside a gated community in order to chase fears away is akin to draining the water out of a pool to make sure that the children can learn to swim in complete safety . . .

40

Tribes and skies

As I have already tried commenting on other people's letters alongside composing my own, let me once more embark on a similar attempt. And, as a matter of fact, for an identical reason: as in the first case, when I discussed *Le silence de Lorna* ('The voice of Lorna's silence'), I feel that the letter I am going to recommend for your close attention (and enjoyment!) is a much sharper and more poignant report from this bizarre liquid modern world of ours than those I write myself, and the story it tells has been composed with a power of the imagination, literary skill and aesthetic beauty of a kind I would hardly be able to match. Such a letter is, I believe, Italo Calvino's short allegorical story *The Tribe with Its Eyes on the Sky*.

The 'tribe' focused on by Calvino, a tribe of coconut gatherers, is – as the title of the story suggests – addicted to 'watching the sky'. The sky it watches obsessively and intensely happens to be a sight that is genuinely fascinating and truly rewarding to watch: it is full of 'new celestial bodies', like jet planes, flying saucers, rockets, and guided missiles . . . While the tribe watches, the tribal witch doctors feel obliged to explain, authoritatively, to their fellow tribesmen the meaning of what they are seeing. They tell the tribesmen that what is currently happening in the sky is a sure sign that the day is fast approaching when the slavery and poverty which has tormented the tribe for centuries will come to an end. Soon 'the barren savannah will bring forth millet and maize', so the tribe will no longer be doomed to feeding itself and surviving, day in, day out, by picking coconuts. And so – here comes the crunch – 'it is hardly worth us racking our brains over new ways of emerging from our present situation; we should trust in the Great Prophecy, rally around its only rightful interpreters, without asking to know more . . .'

Meanwhile, on earth, in that valley where the tribe had built their huts of straw and mud, from which they wandered out daily in search of coconuts and to which they returned, day in, day out, things were also changing. Previously, merchants occasionally arrived in the valley to buy coconuts from the gatherers; the merchants cheated on price, but the clever tribesmen managed to outsmart and fool them time and again, avenging their cheating for good measure. Now, however, the merchants had stopped coming. Instead, an outpost had been opened in the valley by a brand new establishment called Nicer Nut Corporation, whose agents purchased, wholesale, the totality of the coconut crop. The corporation, unlike the old-style travelling traders, allowed no haggling and no opportunities for trickery: prices were fixed in advance, take it or leave it. But, of course, if you 'leave it', you might as well forget your chances of survival until the next batch of coconuts is brought into the valley from picking escapades. On one point, however, the agents of the Nicer Nut Corporation wholeheartedly agree with the tribal witch doctors (and vice versa). They all talk about missiles in the sky and about the news they augur. And the agents, just like the witch doctors, insist that beyond all reasonable doubt 'it is in the power of these shooting stars that our entire destiny lies'.

The teller of the story shares in the destinies and habits of his tribe. Like the rest of the tribe, he spends his evenings at the entrance of his straw and mud hut, closely watching the sky. Like the other tribesmen, he attentively listens to the witch doctors and takes to heart and memorizes what they, and the agents of the Nicer Nut Corporation, keep saying. But he also thinks for himself (or, more precisely, his thoughts think themselves in his mind, without having asked his permission: an idea occurs to him which, he confesses, 'I can't get out of my head'). He thinks that 'a tribe that relies entirely on the will of shooting stars, whatever fortune they may bring, will always sell off its coconuts cheap'.

In another short story, *Beheading the Heads*, Italo Calvino points out that television (here he goes straight to the point, skipping the allegory of a sky filled with shooting stars, 'television' itself being a potent metaphor for so many aspects of our liquid modern life) 'changed a lot of things' – though not necessarily the things which our own, new and improved, technologically sophisticated witch doctors (now renamed 'spin doctors') privately like to pride themselves on having craftily and stealthily changed, while praising television for those changes.

Among things that TV did indeed change, Calvino suggests, is the way we view our leaders (here, 'our leaders' stands for much a larger collection of people who were previously distant and whom we used to hear without seeing, let alone watching: idols, stars, celebrities, all those people we now watch daily, and closely, expecting entertainment, fun and all the illumination and guidance worth getting, and to whom television accords the same treatment as it does to 'our leaders'). Once they were remote figures somewhere high up on the platform, or shown in portraits 'assuming expressions of conventional pride'. Now however, thanks to TV 'everybody can pore over the slightest movements of the features, the irritated twitch of the eyelids under spotlights, the nervous moistening of the lips between one word and another'. In a nutshell, once they arrived so close to us, indeed inside our sitting rooms and bedrooms, our leaders came to appear terribly banal, like the rest of us. And mortal, like the rest of us – that is, arriving only to go away again. Appearing in order to disappear. Clinging to power only to lose it. The sole advantage they seem to have over us, ordinary mortals, is that they are destined for a *public*, not a *private* death – 'the death we are sure to be there for, all together' . . .

Tongue in cheek, though not entirely, Calvino goes as far as suggesting that it is our new awareness of this which explains why, so long as a politician lives, she or he 'will enjoy our interested, anticipatory concern'.

And finally come words so poignant that they deserve to be quoted verbatim and in full:

For us democracy can only begin once we are sure that on the appointed day the television cameras will frame the death throes of our ruling classes to the last man, and then, as an epilogue to the same programme (though many will switch off their sets at this point), the investiture of the new faces who are to rule (and to live) for a similar period.

All that, Calvino concludes, is 'watched by millions of viewers with the serene absorption of one observing the movement of the heavenly bodies in their recurrent circles, a spectacle all the more reassuring the more alien we find it'.

It is, it seems, a custom of more than one tribe, and not necessarily tribes who are remote in space or time, to keep their eyes fixed 'on stars shooting in the sky'. And the reasons why eyes are fixed on stars do not change much from one tribe to another. The consequences of eyes being fixed there do not change much: it is only the equipment serving that activity/passivity that changes. As well as the names of the tribes and of the stars they watch, and the stories told by tribal witch doctors about the meaning of all those shooting stars on which those eyes happen to be fixed. Though not the message of those stories, nor the intentions and purposes of their tellers.

41

Drawing boundaries

In *Les Structures élémentaires de la parenté* (1949),[32] his very first book-length publication, the great French anthropologist Claude Lévi-Strauss selected as the birth-act of culture the prohibition of incest (more exactly, the invention of the *idea* of 'incest': the idea of human intercourse that *can* be performed, but *should not*; of something that is feasible and plausible, and yet forbidden to humans).

Culture, and so the specifically, uniquely human way of being in which the 'ought' is separated from and all too often clashes with the 'is', began with drawing a boundary where there was none. By fencing off certain women as not available for sexual intercourse, women (each of them, like any other woman, 'naturally' and biologically fit for the role of partner in copulation) were 'culturally' divided into those with whom copulation was disallowed, and those with whom it was permitted. Artificial divisions and distinctions imagined and imposed by humans were forced upon natural similarities and differences; more precisely, certain natural traits were injected with added meaning, through associating them with peculiar rules of perception, evaluation and the choice of behavioural pattern.

Since its birth and throughout its long history, culture has followed the same pattern: it has used found or purposively constructed signifiers to divide, distinguish, differentiate, classify and separate objects of perception and evaluation, as well as of the preferred, recommended or enforced modes of responding to those objects. Since its beginning and forever more, culture has consisted and consists in differentiating, 'structuring' and 'regularizing' what would otherwise be uniform, random and volatile. Culture specializes, in other words, in the *management of human choices*.

Boundaries are drawn to *create differences*: differences between one place and the rest of space (for instance, home and 'outside'), between one stretch of time and the rest of time (for instance, childhood and adulthood), between one category of human creature and the rest of humanity (for instance, and most seminally, 'us' and 'them'). Through creating 'differences that make difference', differences calling for the application of different behavioural patterns, probabilities are manipulated: on this or that side of the boundary, certain events become more probable – while others become less likely to happen, perhaps cannot possibly occur. The shapeless mass becomes 'structured' – is given a *structure*. And so we now know where we are, what to expect and what to do. *Borders offer confidence*. They allow us to know how to move, and where and when. They enable us to act with *self-assurance*.

To play that role, borders must be *marked*. There are fences or hedges around your home and other people's homes that simultaneously create and signal the divide between the 'inside' and the 'outside'. There are names stuck to the entry gates or doors that in turn signify the opposition between insiders and outsiders, residents and guests. Obedience to the instructions explicitly spelt out or implied by those signs creates and recreates, manifests and 'naturalizes' an 'orderly world'.

Order, as Mary Douglas memorably explained in her epoch-making study *Purity and Danger* (1966), means the right things in their right places, and nowhere else. It is the boundary that determines which things in which places are 'right' (that is, have the right to be), and which things are 'out of place' where. Bathroom things need to be kept away from the kitchen, bedroom things away from the dining room, outdoor things away from indoor ones. Fried eggs on a breakfast plate may be desirable, but never on your pillow. Well-polished shoes may be welcome, but never on the dinner table. Things out of place are *dirt*. As dirt, they need to be swept away, removed, destroyed or transferred elsewhere, where they 'belong' – if there is a place where they belong, of course (such a place does not always exist, as all state-less refugees and homeless vagabonds will testify). The removal of undesirables is what we call 'cleaning'. What we are engaged in when we put plates on shelves or in cupboards, sweep floors, set tables or make beds is the *preservation or restoration of order*.

In space, boundaries are drawn to create and maintain a *spatial order*: to gather some people and things in certain places and keep other people away from those spaces. Guards at the entrance to shopping malls, restaurants, administrative buildings, 'gated com-munities', theatres or states let some people in while turning away others. They do that by checking tickets, passes, passports and other documents entitling their holders to enter, or by scanning the appearance of those wishing to enter for hints and clues as to their capacities and intentions, and the likelihood that if they are allowed inside they will meet the requirements and expectations that *bona fide* 'insiders' are required and assumed to fulfil. Each model of spatial order divides humans into 'desirables' and 'unde-sirables', under the code names of 'legitimate' (allowed) and 'illegitimate' (not allowed).

And so the prime task of boundaries is to divide; and yet in spite of their primary task and declared purpose, boundaries are not barriers pure and simple – they and those who draw them cannot help also making the borders into *interfaces* joining, connecting and confronting the places they set apart. Boundaries are thereby subjected to opposite, contradictory pressures, turning them into sites of tension and potential objects of contention, antagonism, permanently seething conflict or conflagrations of hostilities.

There are few if any walls without apertures – gates or doors. Walls are, in principle, passable – though, as a rule, the guards on each side of the wall will act at cross-purposes, each trying to make the osmosis, the permeability and penetrability of the bound-ary asymmetrical. The asymmetry is complete or nearly complete in the case of prisons, detention camps and ghettos or 'ghettoized areas' (with Gaza and the West Bank providing the most spectacu-lar current examples), where only one set of armed guards controls passage in both directions; but the notorious 'no-go areas' in cities (dubbed 'mean streets' or 'rough districts') come, or tend to come close to that extreme pattern, juxtaposing the 'we won't go in' attitude of the outsiders with the 'we can't get out' condition of the insiders.

Away from official attention and explicit governmental interference, in the semi-shade, *unmarked* borders at the *grassroots* are currently multiplying. They are side-effects of the increasingly multicultural (diasporic) nature of our urban cohabitation. Fredrik Barth, the eminent Norwegian anthropologist, has noted that contrary to the usual post hoc explanation that borders were drawn and fortified because of striking and potentially dangerous differences between neighbouring populations, the genuine sequence tends to be exactly the opposite: otherwise unnoticeable, small and insignificant, innocuous and irrelevant, or downright imagined and imputed features of neighbours are promoted to the rank of being 'striking' and made relevant because boundaries that have already been drawn yearn for a justification and emotive reinforcement.

We can add, however, that the 'grassroots', 'immaterial' and only mentally, not sensually, noticeable borders, formed by the avoidance of sharing goods, sharing meals and sharing beds, rather than by trenches, bunkers, watch towers, concrete or barbed wire, perform a double function: alongside the function of separation, prompted by fear of the unknown and desire for security, there is the role or destiny of an 'interface': encounter, exchange, and in the end a fusion of cognitive horizons and daily practices. It is here, at this 'microsocial' level of face-to-face encounters, that different traditions, beliefs, cultural inspirations and lifestyles – which governmentally supervised and administered borders at the 'macrosocial' level struggle, with mixed success, to keep apart – meet at close quarters and point blank, share daily life and inevitably enter a dialogue – peaceful and benevolent, or antagonistic and stormy, but always leading towards familiarization and less estrangement – and so potentially to mutual understanding, respect and solidarity.

In our liquid modern world the complex task of working out the conditions for an agreeable and mutually beneficial method for different (and determined to remain different) forms of life to cohabit has been dumped on (principally urban) localities – as with so many other globally produced problems – making them with or without their consent into willing or unwilling laboratories in which the ways and means of human cohabitation on a globalized planet can be discovered or invented, experimented with, subjected to practical tests and eventually learned. Intercommunal (more precisely, interdiasporic) frontiers (material or mental, made of bricks and mortar or symbolic) are occasionally battlefields where common, multisourced apprehensions and frustrations are unloaded, but they are also, less spectacularly but more consistently and seminally, creative workshops for the art of cohabitation; plots in which the seeds of future forms of humanity are (knowingly or not) sown and sprout.

Nothing in history is predetermined; history is a trace left on time by multiple, dispersed and disparate human choices, seldom if ever coordinated. It is much too early to foresee which of the two interrelated functions of borders will eventually prevail. Of one thing we can be pretty sure, though: we (and our children) will lie on the beds that we, collectively, are making for ourselves (and for them). And through drawing borders and negotiating the norms of life on the frontierland, those beds *are* made. Knowingly or not, by design or by default, purposefully or inadvertently . . . Whether we want it, or not.

How good people turn evil

The title chosen for this letter is the subtitle of Philip Zimbardo's book *The Lucifer Effect*[33] – a blood-curdling and nerve-racking study of a bunch of good, ordinary, liked and likeable American lads and lasses who turned into monsters once they were transported to the faraway country of Iraq and put in charge of prisoners charged with ill intentions and suspected to belong to an inferior brand of humans or be somewhat less than human.

How safe and comfortable, cosy and friendly the world would feel if it were monsters and monsters alone who perpetrated monstrous deeds. Against monsters we are fairly well protected, and so we may be assured that we are insured against the evil deeds that monsters are capable of and threaten to perpetrate. We have psychologists to spot psychopaths and sociopaths, we have sociologists to tell us where they are likely to crop up, propagate and congregate, we have judges to condemn them to confinement and isolation, and police or psychiatrists to make sure they stay there.

Alas, the good, ordinary, likeable American lads and lasses were not monsters. If they had not been assigned to lord it over the inmates of Abu Ghraib, we would never know (surmise, guess, imagine, fantasize) what they were capable of doing. It wouldn't occur to any of us that the smiling girl at the counter might, once on overseas assignment, excel at devising ever more clever and fanciful, as well as wicked and perverse, tricks to harass, molest, torture and dehumanize her wards. In her and her companions' hometowns, their neighbours refuse to believe to this very day that those lads and lasses they have known since their childhood are the same folks as the monsters in the snapshots of the Abu Ghraib torture chambers. But they are.

In the conclusion of his protracted and thorough psychological study of Chip Frederick, the suspected leader and guide of the torturers' pack, Philip Zimbardo had to say that

> there is absolutely nothing in his record that I was able to uncover that would predict that Chip Frederick would engage in any form of abusive, sadistic behavior. On the contrary, there is much in his record to suggest that had he not been forced to work and live in such an abnormal situation, he might have been the military's All-American poster soldier on its recruitment ads.[34]

Indeed, Chip Frederick would have passed any imaginable psychological test with flying colours, as well as the kind of thorough scrutiny of his behavioural record routinely applied in selecting candidates for the most responsible and ethically sensitive services, like for instance those of the official guardians of law and order . . .

In the case of Chip Frederick and his closest and most notorious companion, Lynndie England, you might still insist (even if counterfactually) that they had acted on command and had been forced to engage in atrocities they detested and abhorred – meek sheep rather than predatory wolves. The sole charge against them you might then approve of would be that of cowardice or exaggerated respect for their superiors; at the utmost, the charge of too easily abandoning the moral principles which guided them in 'ordinary' life. But what about those at the top of the bureaucratic ladder? Those who gave commands, forced obedience and punished the disobedient? Those people, surely, must have been monsters?

The inquiry into the Abu Ghraib atrocity never reached the top echelons of the American military command; for those top people to be brought to trial and tried for war crimes, they would first need to find themselves in the camp of the defeated in the war they waged. But Adolf Eichmann, presiding over the tools and procedures of the 'final solution' of the 'Jewish problem' and giving orders to their operators, was in that camp, had been captured by victors and brought to their courts. There was an occasion, therefore, to submit the 'monster hypothesis' to a most careful, indeed meticulous scrutiny – and by the most distinguished members of the psychological and psychiatric professions. The final conclusion drawn from that most thorough and reliable research was anything but ambiguous. Here it is, as conveyed by Hannah Arendt:

> Half a dozen psychiatrists had certified him as 'normal' – 'More normal, at any rate, than I am after examining him', one of them was said to have exclaimed, while another had found his whole psychological outlook, his attitude towards wife and children, mother and father, brothers, sisters and friends was 'not only normal but most desirable'.
>
> . . .
>
> The trouble with Eichmann was precisely that so many were like him, and that the many were neither perverted nor sadistic, that they were, and still are, terribly and terrifyingly normal. From the viewpoint of our legal institutions and our moral standards of judgment, this normality was much more terrifying than all the atrocities put together . . .[35]

It must indeed have been more terrifying: if normal people (one is tempted to add: 'like you and me'), and not monsters, commit atrocities and are capable of acting in a perverted and sadistic way, than all the sieves we've invented to strain out the carriers of inhumanity from the rest of the human species are either faulty or downright misconceived, and most certainly ineffective. And so we are, to cut a long story short, unprotected (one is tempted to add: 'defenceless against our own morbid capacity'). Employing their ingenuity to the utmost and trying as hard as they could to 'civilize' human manners and the patterns of human togetherness, our ancestors, and also those of us who follow their line of thought and action, are barking so to speak up the wrong tree . . .

Fits of sadism and paroxysms of bestiality may occur in anybody. If Eichmann was 'normal', then no one is *a priori* exempt from suspicion. None of our dazzlingly normal friends and acquaintances. Neither are we. Chip Fredericks and Adolf Eichmanns walk in our streets in full view, queue at shopping checkouts, fill cinemas and football grandstands, travel on trains and city buses. They might even live next door, or sit at our dining table. All of them, given propitious circumstances, might do what Chip Frederick and Adolf Eichmann did. And what about me?! Since so many people can potentially commit acts of humanity, I might easily, by chance, become one of their victims. *They* can do it. But equally easily I may yet prove to be one of 'them': another 'normal person' who can do it to others . . .

John M. Steiner coined the notion of a 'sleeper' to denote a personal inclination to commit violence, that is hypothetically present in an individual while still remaining invisible – an inclination that can (is bound to?) surface under certain, propitious conditions:[36] presumably once the factors that hitherto repressed it and kept it under cover are abruptly weakened or removed. Ervin Staub moved one (gigantic) step further, removing the references to 'particularity' in Steiner's proposition and hypothesizing the presence of malevolent 'sleepers' in most, perhaps all humans: 'Evil . . . committed by ordinary people is the norm, not an exception.'[37] Is he right? We don't know and will never know, at least know for sure, as there is no way empirically to prove or disprove that guess.

What do we know for sure? The ease, As Zimbardo himself found in his earlier experiments conducted at Stanford University with people randomly selected to play the role of 'prison guards' towards other people (also randomly) selected for the role and situation of prisoners, 'with which sadistic behaviour could be elicited in individuals who were not "sadistic types".'[38] Or, as Stanley Milgram found in his Harvard experiments with people again randomly selected who were asked to inflict a series of what they were made to believe were painful electrical shocks of escalating magnitude: that 'obedience to authority', any authority, regardless of the nature of the commands that authority may give, even if the subjects are commanded to commit actions they find repugnant and revolting, is a 'deeply ingrained behaviour tendency'.[39] If you add to that such well-nigh universal sediments of socialization as the attributes of loyalty, sense of duty and discipline, 'men are led to kill with little difficulty'.

It is easy, in other words, to prod non-evil people to commit evil things. Christopher R. Browning investigated the convoluted yet invariably gory itinerary of the men belonging to the German Reserve Police Battalion 101, conscripted into the police from among adults unfit for frontline duty and assigned to participate in the mass murder of Jews in Poland.[40] Those people, who had never been known to commit violent, let alone murderous acts before, and were not suspected of being capable of committing them, were ready (not all of them, but a considerable majority) to comply with the command to murder: shoot men and women, old people and children, all unarmed and obviously innocent since they had not been charged with any crime, and none of them nestling the slightest intention to harm them or their comrades-in-arms. What Browning found, however (publishing it under the telling title of *Ordinary Men*), was that about 10 to 20 per cent of the policemen asked to be excused from carrying out the orders. There was 'a nucleus of increasingly enthusiastic killers who vol- unteered for the firing squads and "Jew hunts"; a larger group of policemen who performed as shooters and ghetto clearers when assigned but who did not seek opportunities to kill (and in some cases refrained from killing . . .); and a small group (less than 20 percent) of refusers and evaders'. The most striking aspect of that finding was that the statistical distribution of zealots, refusers and the 'neither-nor' proved to be amazingly similar to that of the reactions to the authoritatively endorsed commands by the sub- jects of Zimbardo's and Milgram's experiments. In all cases, some were only too eager to exploit the situation in order to give vent to their evil drives; some – roughly of the same number – refused to do evil whatever the circumstances; whereas an extensive 'middle ground' was filled by people who were indifferent, luke- warm and not particularly engaged or strongly committed to one or other side of the attitudinal spectrum – avoiding taking a stand and preferring instead to follow the line of least resistance and do whatever prudence dictated and unconcern allowed them to do at the time.

In other words, in all three cases (and possibly in innumerable other cases in the category of which these three studies have been acclaimed as the most spectacular and convincing examples), the distribution of the probability that the command to do evil will be obeyed has followed the rule known in statistics as the Gaussian curve (sometimes called the Gaussian bell, distribution or function) – believed to be the graph of the most common, to wit 'normal', distribution of probabilities. We read in Wikipedia that what the notion of the Gaussian curve refers to is the tendency of results to 'cluster around a mean or average'. 'The graph of the associated probability density function is bell-shaped, with a peak at the mean.' We also read that 'by the central limit theorem, any variable that is the sum of a large number of independent factors is likely to be normally distributed'.

As the probabilities of various behavioural responses by people exposed to pressure to do evil show a clear tendency to take the form of a Gaussian curve, we can risk the supposition that, in their case as well, the result was caused by the mutual interference of a *large* number of *independent* factors. Commands descending from on high, instinctual or deeply entrenched respect for, or fear of, authority, loyalty reinforced by considerations of duty and/or by drilled discipline were some of them; but not necessarily the only ones.

It seems plausible that under the conditions of liquid modernity, marked by a loosening or dissipation of bureaucratic hierarchies of authority as well as by a multiplication of the 'sites from which authoritative recommendations are voiced', two factors responsible for a relative weakening and diminished audibility of those voices, other (more individual, idiosyncratic and personal) factors, for instance character (to be discussed in the next letter), may play an increasingly important role. The humanity of humans would surely gain if they did.

43

Fate and character

'How can we act without fear of a blunder and the risk of incon-sequentiality inevitably contained in every protest?' Was what I was asked by Martina, one of *La Repubblica*'s readers. My answer, the only answer I could responsibly offer, was: alas, we can't . . .

We cannot be sure before we act that mistakes won't be made, and we can't be certain in advance that by the end of the day we will have been proved to be up to the task. Protesting is not the only kind of activity to which this rule applies. There are few if any foolproof, totally reliable recipes for action, 'success guaran-teed, or your money back' – and the more important our actions are for ourselves and others, the more uncertain (indeed, impos-sible to predict) will, by and large, their results be. Unlike when you try to open a tin with the 'new and improved' gadget you've just bought, there are no instructions attached to life choices that can just be read point by point and followed point by point. To live is to take risks. Or, to extend the memorable verdict on love by the Roman poet Lucan: to live, as to love, means giving hostages to fate.

Will such a life be uncomfortable, unnerving, even frightening? Yes, indeed, it may be – it is bound to be. The snag is that there is no other life to live. As Michel Foucault suggested, we are bound to *create* our life itinerary, and in the course of creating it also to create ourselves – just as *works of art* are *created* by artists. The course of life, its 'overall purpose', its 'ultimate destination', can only be, and indeed is and forever will remain, a 'do-it-yourself job'. These days each man and each woman is a life artist not so much by choice as, so to speak, *by decree of universal fate*. And that means that non-action also counts as action; placidly accepting the world and thus cooperating in the wrongdoings piling up to which we object in words is also a choice – just like our protest and active resistance against the iniquities endemic in the way of life the world presses us to obediently follow. Life cannot be anything but a work of art, if it is a *human* life – a life of a human being, that is, a being endowed with will and freedom of choice.

The most powerful minds of the modern era and legions of their followers agreed in selecting Socrates, the ancient sage and restless spirit who never relented in his search for truth, nobility and beauty, as a model for a life well chosen: a model for a life that is meaningful, dignified, worthy of living and praiseworthy. Moreover, they all did it for much the same reason: they chose Socrates because this ancient sage and forefather of modern thought was fully and truly (and above all self-consciously!) a 'self-made man', a pastmaster of self-creation and self-assertion – and yet he never presented the way of being he himself chose and indefatigably followed as the universally valid model of the *only* worthy way of life, that is, as a model which all other humans ought for that reason to emulate. For the great modern philosophers who recommended Socrates' life as a pattern for making one's own, to 'imitate Socrates' meant to compose, knowingly, *one's own* self, personality and/or identity, and to do this freely and autonomously; *not* to copy the personality Socrates had created for himself, or for that matter any other personality, whoever might have composed it. What mattered was *self*-definition and *self*-assertion, the readiness to accept that life *is* and *must be* a work of art, for whose merits and shortcomings the life's 'auctor' (actor and author rolled into one, the designer and simultaneously executor of the design) bears full responsibility. 'To imitate Socrates' meant in other words to *refuse to imitate* the person 'Socrates', or for that matter any other person – to reject heteronomy, imitation, duplicating, copying *as such*. The model of life Socrates selected for himself, painstakingly composed and laboriously cultivated against all odds (even in the end putting his own death by poison above the prospect of its surrender), might have suited his kind of person perfectly, but it would not necessarily suit all those who made a point of 'being *like* Socrates'. A slavish emulation of the specific mode of life constructed by Socrates, and to which he remained unhesitatingly, steadfastly loyal, would amount to a *betrayal* of his legacy and an act of *rejection* of his message, which was first and foremost about individual *autonomy* and individual *responsibility*. Imitation perfectly suits a copying machine, but will never result in the *original* artistic creation that (Socrates suggested) human life should strive to become.

All artists struggle with the resistance of the material on which they wish to engrave their visions. All works of art bear the traces of that struggle – of its victories and defeats, and the many enforced, though no less shameful for that reason, compromises. Artists of life and their works are no exceptions to that rule. The chisels used by artists of life (knowingly or not, and with greater or lesser skill) in their engraving efforts are their *characters*. Thomas Hardy referred to that when he declared that 'the fate of man is his character'. *Fate*, and accidents, its guerrilla troops, decide the range of choices confronting the artists of life. But it is their *characters* that decide what choices the artists of life will make.

In her milestone study *When Light Pierced the Darkness*, sociologist Nechama Tec reported the results of her scrutiny of factors that inclined some witnesses of the Holocaust to save the lives of its appointed victims at the cost of risking their own. Tec carefully calculated statistical correlations between willingness to help and readiness for self-sacrifice, and all the factors commonly assumed to determine human behaviour, such as social milieu and class, level of education, wealth, religious creed and political denomination – but she found no correlation. There was, it appeared, no 'statistically significant' factor *determining* moral choices. Statistically, the people who helped did not differ from the rest of the population, even if the moral value of their conduct and the human significance of its consequences differed most radically from the most common, majority responses.

So why did the helpers risk joining the ranks of the victims, rather than lock their doors and lower their blinds to avoid the sight of their suffering? The only answer is that the helpers, unlike most other people of the same social class, education, religious faith or political loyalties, *could not behave differently*. Just could not. Saving their own physical safety and comfort could not make up for the spiritual distress caused by the sight of people suffering and by the pangs of wounded conscience. They would probably never have forgiven themselves for putting their own welfare before those whom they could have saved, but refused or neglected to do so.

Fate and accidents beyond the actor's control make some choices more probable than others. Character, however, defies those statistical probabilities. It deprives fate and accidents of the omnipotence they are believed or claim to possess. Between resigned acceptance and a bold decision to defy the force of circumstances stands character. It is an actor's character that submits choices which have triumphantly passed the tests of *probability* or *plausibility* to another test, immensely more demanding and much less ready for compromise and patient with excuses: the test of *moral acceptability*. It was his character that impelled Martin Luther on 31 October 1517, the eve of All Saints, to declare 'Ich kann nicht anders' (I cannot do otherwise) when he dared to affix his 95 heretical theses to the door of the Castle Church in Wittenberg.

44

Albert Camus

Or: *I* rebel, therefore *we* exist . . .

Half a century has passed without Albert Camus's poignant, nagging and prodding, provoking and invigorating comments. In all that time the library of books, studies and essays dedicated to the author of *L'Étranger*, *La Peste*, *La Chute* and *Le Premier Homme* has swelled unstoppably: by 1 October 2009, Questia, the 'online library of books and journals' most frequently consulted by academics, had listed 3,171 items, including 2,528 of book size, discussing his ideas and their place in the history of thought; Google Books, a website with a still wider audience, counted 9,953. Most of the authors of the books and articles had struggled ultimately with one question: what sort of stand would Albert Camus have taken were he to have witnessed the world – our world – that came into being after his untimely death: what would his comments, appeals and advice have been like, the ones he had no time to offer us and which we so sorely miss.

One question, many answers, many *different* answers . . . And no wonder. About Franz Kafka, Camus opined: 'Tout l'art de Kafka est d'obliger le lecteur à relire' ('All Kafka's art is in obliging the reader to read again'). Why? His (Kafka's) solutions or their absence suggest explications, but ones 'qui ne sont pas révélées en clair' (that 'are not clearly revealed'); to clarify them, one would need to do nothing less than reread history 'sous un nouvel angle' ('from a novel perspective'). In other words, Kafka's art is to avoid the temptation to try to embrace the unembraceable and to close issues bound to stay forever open, intriguing and enervating – and so never to cease to question and provoke the reader, while inspiring and beefing up his or her efforts at rethinking. Thanks to that peculiarity, Kafka's inspirations never die; let me suggest that the controversies and contentions those inspirations continue to beget are as close as can be conceived to what the alchemists dreamt of as the 'philosopher's stone', from which the 'elixir of life' could be drawn, forever and ever. In his portrait of Kafka, Camus sketched the model of all immortal thoughts: that trademark of all great thinkers, including himself . . .

I wouldn't dare to pretend that I've managed (or even earnestly tried) to study the thousands of reinterpretations that Camus's legacy has begotten to date. I lack therefore the competence to summarize, let alone to evaluate, the state of the ongoing debate, let alone to predict its further course. In the comments that follow, I am bound to limit myself to *my* Camus: to my reading of Camus, and to the sound of his voice listened to once more, 50 and more years later, this time through the commotion and uproar of our liquid modern bazaar; in short, to the author of, primarily, *Le Mythe de Sisyphe* and *L'Homme révolté*, two books that like few others read in my youth helped me to come to terms with the oddities and absurdities of the world we inhabit – and which we continue to make, day in, day out, consciously or not, through the mode of our habitation. I won't be surprised if other avid readers of Camus and seekers of his message to posterity find my reading different from theirs, odd or even perverse. While searching indefatigably for the truth of the human predicament, Camus was careful to follow the object of his exploration in its openness to a variety of explications and judgements – and staunchly resisted any premature foreclosure of the matter (any foreclosure, in the case of the impenetrable mystery of human nature and potential, has to be premature), while shunning every temptation to cleanse his portrayal of the human plight – for the sake of the logic and clarity of his narrative – from the ambiguity and ambivalence that are its irreducible, perhaps defining, attributes. Camus's definition of the intellectual was, let's recall, 'someone whose mind watches itself' . . .

Several years ago I was asked by an interviewer 'to summarize my concerns in a paragraph'. I could not find a better shorthand description of the purpose of a sociologist's effort to explore and record the convoluted paths of human experience than a sentence borrowed from Camus: 'There is beauty and there are the humiliated. Whatever difficulties the enterprise may present, I should like never to be unfaithful either to the second or the first.' Many a radical and self-confident writer of recipes for happy people would decry that profession of faith as a blameworthy invitation to straddle the barricade. Camus has shown, however, in my view beyond reasonable doubt, that 'taking sides' and sacrificing one of those two tasks for the sake of (apparently) better fulfilling the other will inevitably end in casting *both* tasks beyond reach. Camus placed himself, in his own words, 'half way between misery and the sun': 'Misery kept me', he explained, 'from believing that all was well under the sun, and the sun taught me that history wasn't everything.' Camus confessed to being 'pessimistic as to human history, optimistic as to man' – man being, as he insisted, 'the only creature that refuses to be what he is'. Man's freedom, Camus pointed out, 'is nothing other than a chance to be better' – and 'the only way to deal with an un-free world is to become so absolutely free that your very existence is an act of rebellion'.

Camus's portrayal of human destiny and prospects is located somewhere betwixt and between the likenesses of Sisyphus and Prometheus, struggling – in vain, yet obstinately and indefatigably – towards a reunion and merger of the two. Prometheus, the hero of *L'Homme révolté*, chooses life-for-*others*, a life-of-rebellion-against *their* misery, as the solution of that 'absurdity of the human condition' that drew Sisyphus, overwhelmed by and preoccupied with *his own* misery, towards suicide as the sole answer to and escape from his human, all-too-human plight (faithful to the ancient wisdom spelled out by Pliny the Elder, presumably for the use of all practitioners of *amour-de-soi* coupled with *amour propre*: 'Amid the miseries of our life on earth, suicide is God's best gift to man'). In Camus's juxtaposition of Sisyphus and Prometheus, refusal was made in the name of affirmation: 'I rebel', as Camus would conclude, 'therefore we exist.' It is as though humans invented logic, harmony, order and *Eindeutigkeit* (non-ambiguity) as their ideals only to be prompted, by their predicament and their choices, to defy each one of them through their practice . . . 'We' won't be conjured up by a lonely Sisyphus with a stone, a slope and a self-defeating task as his sole company.

But even within the apparently hopeless and prospectless plight of Sisyphus, faced as he is with the utter absurdity of his existence, there is room, an abominably tiny bit of room to be sure, but wide enough all the same for Prometheus to step into it. Sisyphus's lot is tragic only because it is conscious, aware of the ultimate sense-lessness of his labours. But, as Camus explains, 'La clairvoyance qui devait faire son tourment consomme du même coup sa victoire. Il n'est pas de destin qui ne se surmonte par le mépris'[41] ('The perceptiveness that should have been his agony by the same token accomplishes his victory. There is no fate that can't be overcome by disdain'). Pushing morbid self-awareness away and opening himself to Prometheus's visit, Sisyphus may yet turn from a tragic figure of a slave-to-things into their joyous *doer*. 'Happiness and the absurd', Camus points out, 'are two sons of the same earth. They are inseparable.' And he adds: to Sisyphus, this universe 'without a master' seems 'neither sterile nor futile. Each atom of that stone, each mineral flake of that night-filled mountain, in itself forms a world. The struggle itself toward the heights is enough to fill a man's heart. *One must imagine Sisyphus happy*' (emphasis added). Sisyphus is reconciled to the world as it is, and that act of acceptance paves the way to rebellion; indeed, it makes rebellion, if not inescapable, then at least the most likely outcome.

That combination of acceptance and rebellion, of concern with and care for beauty and concern and care for the miserable, are meant to protect Camus's project on both fronts: against a resignation pregnant with suicidal impulses, and a self-assurance pregnant with indifference to the human cost of revolt. Camus tells us that revolt, revolution and striving for freedom are inevitable aspects of human existence, but that we must set and watch their limits to avoid these admirable pursuits ending in tyranny.

Was it indeed 50 years ago that Camus died?

Notes

1 *Guardian Weekend*, 4 and 11 Aug. 2007.
2 See 'The thoughtful', *FO/futureorientation*, Jan. 2008, p. 11.
3 At www.wxii12.com/health/16172076/detail.html.
4 See Michel Foucault, *The History of Sexuality*, vol. 1, trans. Robert Hurley (Penguin, 1978), pp. 42ff.
5 See 'Les victimes de violences sexuelles en parlent de plus en plus', *Le Monde*, 30 May 2008.
6 Frank Furedi, 'Thou shalt not hug', *New Statesman*, 26 June 2008.
7 Neal Lawson, *All Consuming* (Penguin, 2009).
8 Georg Simmel, 'Zur Psychologie der Mode; Soziologische Studie', in *Gesamtausgabe*, vol. 5 (Suhrkamp, 1992).
9 Zygmunt Bauman, *The Art of Life* (Polity, 2008).
10 Andy McSmith, 'Cultural elite does not exist, academics claim', at www.independent.co.uk, 20 Dec. 2007.
11 See R. A. Petersen and A. Simkus, 'How musical tastes mark occupational status groups', in M. Lamont and M. Fournier (eds), *Cultivating Differences: Symbolic Boundaries and the Making of Inequality* (University of Chicago Press, 1992).
12 See his summary of, and illuminating reflection on, two decades of his own and related studies in 'Changing arts audiences: capitalizing on omnivorousness', presented at a workshop on 14 Oct. 2005. At culturalpolicy.uchicago.edu.
13 See Philip French, 'A hootenanny New Year to all', the *Observer* television supplement, 30 Dec. 2007–5 Jan. 2008, p. 6.
14 Richard Wilkinson and Kate Pickett, *The Spirit Level* (Allen Lane, 2009).

15 See Göran Therborn, 'The killing fields of inequality', *Soundings* (Summer 2009), pp. 20–32.
16 Richard Rorty, *Philosophy and Social Hope* (Penguin, 1999), pp. 203–4.
17 See Italo Calvino, *Invisible Cities* (Secker and Warburg, 1974).
18 Luc Boltanski and Eve Chiapello, *The New Spirit of Capitalism* (Verso, 2005).
19 Ulrich Beck, *Weltrisikogesellshaft* (Suhrkamp, 2007). Here quoted after Ciaran Cronin's translation, *World at Risk* (Polity, 2009), pp. 4–6.
20 John Gray, *Gray's Anatomy: Selected Writings* (Allen Lane, 2009), pp. 223, 236.
21 In *Quaderni del carcere*; here quoted after Antonio Gramsci, *Selections from the Prison Notebooks*, ed. and trans. Quintin Hoare and Geoffrey Nowell-Smith (Lawrence and Wishart, 1971), p. 276.
22 See Keith Tester, 'Pleasure, reality, the novel and pathology', *Journal of Anthropological Psychology*, no. 21 (2009), pp. 23–6.
23 Gray, *Gray's Anatomy*, p. 231.
24 Roberto Toscano and Ramin Jahanbegloo, *Beyond Violence: Principles for an Open Century* (Har-Anand, 2009), p. 78.
25 See Mark Furlong, 'Crying to be heard', *Overland*, no. 194 (22 Mar. 2009).
26 Serge Latouche, *Farewell to Growth* (Polity, 2009).
27 In Furlong, 'Crying to be heard'.
28 Naomi Klein, 'Obama's big silence', *Guardian Weekend*, 12 Sept. 2009.
29 Jonathan Rutherford, *After Identity* (Lawrence and Wishart, 2007), pp. 59–60.
30 Richard Sennett, *The Uses of Disorder: Personal Identity and City Life* (Faber, 1996), pp. 39, 42.
31 Anna Minton, Ground Control (Penguin, 2009).
32 In English as Claude Lévi-Strauss, *The Elementary Structures of Kinship* (Beacon Press, 1969).
33 Philip Zimbardo, *The Lucifer Effect* (Rider, 2007).
34 Ibid., p. 344.
35 Hannah Arendt, *Eichmann in Jerusalem* (Penguin, 1994), pp. 25–6, 276.
36 See John M. Steiner, 'The SS yesterday and today: a sociopsychological view', in: Joel E. Dimsdale (ed.), *Survivors, Victims, Perpetrators* (Hemisphere, 1982).
37 Ervin Staub, *The Roots of Evil* (Cambridge University Press, 1989), p. 126.

38 Craig Haney, Curtis Banks and Philip Zimbardo, 'Interpersonal dynamics in a simulated prison', *International Journal of Criminology and Penology*, 1 (1983), pp. 69–97.
39 Stanley Milgram, *Obedience to Authority: An Experimental View* (repr. Harper, 2009).
40 Christopher R. Browning, *Ordinary Men* (Penguin, 2001).
41 See Albert Camus, *The Myth of Sisyphus* (Penguin, 2005).

70,-